PRAISE FOR *THRIVE*

"It gives me great pleasure to strongly endorse this outstanding book written by Luke McKenna, who as an experienced educator has tapped into his extensive knowledge of school culture, to provide a clear and constructive narrative about some of the key barriers to students achieving personal excellence and how to address these effectively. What the text conveys is Luke's passion for making a difference in the lives of young people, which is a common driver for educators across the globe. Teachers and parents can easily fall into the trap of limiting our expectations for students and Luke provides practical advice to address this issue through intelligently reviewing the educational research and highlighting common themes. He has thrown out the challenge to educators to refocus on what really matters and his articulation of the importance of a growth mindset, grit (persistence and resilience) and well-being will resonate with educators. All school leaders want every student in their care to thrive, how best to achieve this is the admirable focus of this work."

— **Stephen Webber, Headmaster, Guildford Grammar School.**

"Luke has focused on the essence of our development and success – our attitude and how it impacts our lives. In times where technology and social norms are centred on less face-to-face contact and on more instantaneous feedback, our ability to think far and wide into the future is governed by the way we think now which influences our subsequent actions. Luke has illustrated how, as parents and educators, we can assist our children to develop the skills that will enhance their success and live productive, happy lives. This is a resource that schools, parents or anyone dealing with young people should read and instigate. Insightful, practical and relevant."

— **Brett Harvey, CEO, Coaction Consultancy. 22 Years in Education.**

"This book intelligently combines current research and invaluable experience to identify the important factors that children and adolescents need to thrive in today's society. Luke understands the significance of social and emotional well being on school performance and life after school."

— Stephen Morton, Principal Psychologist, Brisbane Child and Adolescent Psychology Centre

"As an educator for over 25 years, I am constantly amazed by the enormous ability of young people. When we present opportunities for them to shine, they invariably succeed and amaze us. However, I have always thought we still fall way short of the mark in terms of tapping into their vast store of potential. Various barriers often restrict what they are capable of becoming – stress, anxiety, poor self belief and the assumption that we are born with a particular set of skills and abilities which we can't change. Luke provides us with the theory and evidence we need to remove these barriers and unlock the potential that often lay dormant within our young people. *Thrive* provides us with the tools necessary to unleash potential and enable our students to develop a growth mindset that gives them the much needed confidence to know they can learn new skills and overcome perceived limitations in their learning. This change in mindset is the key to greater personal resilience, which in turn will reduce the prevalence of serious mental health issues which severely inhibits growth.

Thrive encapsulates Luke's passion and commitment to improving the lives of our students by helping them to see that they are far more capable than they realise, and highlights the importance of a far broader view of education; one that goes beyond academic education to include vital social and emotional learning which is essential for people to cope in our increasingly complex world."

— Steve Centra, Principal, Lumen Christi College.

"Valuable reading for educators and parents alike. Luke MCKenna's interpretation and perspective on student development maps a clear pathway that can enable students to develop successful learning skills and maximise their potential."

— **Tony Nicholson, Director of Academic Excellence, Helensvale State High School.**

"Passion, dedication and persistence are evident in children who are best able to cultivate their intelligence and talents. This text presents both a credible summary of the science behind guiding children to thrive, and also a range of practical strategies to help parents and teachers assist children on their life journey. This book is about understanding and application and particularly turning proven theory in proven practice."

— **Dr Ken Avenell, Principal Education Officer – Professional Learning, Formation and Leadership, Brisbane Catholic Education.**

"As principal of a primary school, I have been concerned for a number of years of the mental blocks that students develop which inhibit their learning. In this book, McKenna draws upon the latest research about how we learn and presents an informative and practical guide on how social emotional learning contributes greatly to improving student learning. It is a 'must read' book for all educators and parents who want students to thrive at school. It is also a great book for anyone who wants to get more out of life and make a real positive difference to the people they live and work with. I commend McKenna on drawing a number of important ideas together in this book: growth mindset, grit and wellbeing. I would highly recommend it for anyone who educates students."

— **Peter Pashen, Principal, All Saints Primary School.**

THRIVE

UNLOCKING THE TRUTH ABOUT STUDENT PERFORMANCE

A practical guide for
educators and parents

LUKE MCKENNA

Catalogue-in-Publication details available on request from the National Library of Australia.

ISBN: 978-0-9943866-0-1 (pbk)

Edited by Angela Slade

Typesetting and design by Publicious P/L
www.publicious.com.au

Book cover image: © Thaut Images - Fotolia.com

Published with the assistance of Publicious P/L
www.publicious.com.au

To my wonderful wife, Laura. For all of your support, commitment and love- not only during this process, but always. Thank you.

To my boys Elijah and Oscar. You mean the world to me. You are the inspiration for my work in trying to help people to thrive.

CONTENTS

PART FOUR: WELLBEING

PART FIVE: EFFECTIVE SCHOOL IMPLEMENTATION

ABOUT THE AUTHOR

Unleashing Personal Potential founder, Luke McKenna, is an educator who specialises in working with schools to build growth mindsets, resilience and wellbeing for all students. Over the last 10 years, he has worked as a classroom teacher and school administrator.

This experience has given Luke insight into some of the inhibitors to learning that exist for many of the students currently in our schools. It is this knowledge, and his passion for empowering people to live to their full potential that led Luke to establish Unleashing Personal Potential (UPP) in 2014. Drawing from the best currently available research, UPP has built a solid foundation around the science of cultivating student potential – particularly around the topics of growth mindsets, grit and wellbeing.

Since establishing UPP, Luke has worked with educators and students across Australian primary and secondary schools from the independent, Catholic and public sectors. He holds degrees in Business and Education, as well as a Masters of Educational Leadership. His work has also been published in the *Australian Journal of Middle Schooling*.

He lives in Brisbane with his wife, Laura, and their two young children.

INTRODUCTION

Thrive:
1. To grow vigorously; to flourish:
2. To be successful or make steady progress; to prosper. (American Heritage® Dictionary of the English Language, 2011)

Don't we all want our young people to thrive? As teachers, we hope our students will thrive. As parents, we hope our children will thrive. Any educator who has been in and around schools for a length of time will notice some obvious differences between students who seem to be thriving and students who are just scraping through. Some of the factors that lead to thriving can be taught and they can be learned. This book will seek to explore the "big three" factors that lead to thriving young people in our schools – growth mindsets, grit and wellbeing.

During my time spent in schools, it has become clear that there are some distinct and obvious differences between those who thrive and those who don't. Thriving can be learned by all students, but it can only be learned if it is taught. Ultimately, don't we want to be part of a society where our young people are learning and thriving? A society in which adults thrive throughout their lives due to the skills they learned at school.

There are a small number of our best teachers and parents who are already aware of these factors and are committed to changing the hearts and minds of the young people in their care. There are a large proportion of teachers and parents who care about young people and are committed to doing what they can to assist, and are looking for some direction.

It is my hope that this book will raise the awareness of many more educators and parents around the three key factors that lead to personal thriving. If this interests you, practical strategies and resources to support and assist schools can be found at www. unleashingpersonalpotential.com.au.

This book draws on the best currently available evidence from the fields of psychology, education and neuroscience and relates it in practical ways for educators and parents. I have taken the "goldilocks" approach, ensuring that when it comes to the research – it is not too heavy (as to become burdensome), and not too light (as to carry little reliability or credibility). Hopefully, you will find that it is just right- the perfect balance of theory and real-world experience (Barber, 2011).

This book is proactive in nature, rather than reactive. Rather than try to fix issues and problems, it is focused on empowering people to live to their full potential. It is not about surviving; it is about thriving. While I have identified three fundamental factors that are major inhibitors to human thriving, the majority of this work is about equipping educators and parents with the research, ideas and tools to enhance thriving. My work in schools focuses on unleashing potential by developing school communities that flourish. In other words, this book is about equipping school communities so that young people gain the knowledge, understanding and skills that enable them to thrive.

I am of the belief that, regardless of our age or level of experience, we are all capable of learning. In fact, research in neuroscience tells us that we are capable of learning from the "cradle to the grave".

Unfortunately, it seems to me that some people stopped learning long ago. As you read the book and think about your children or students, occasionally pause for reflection about the application of the content for your own life. You will be the best educator and parent you can possibly be when you have internalised the content, rather than memorised it. After all, "first we teach who we are", then we teach what we know (Palmer, 1998). Much of the content is as relevant to adults as it is to students.

So, join me on the journey of continuous learning and equip the young people in your life with the knowledge and skills they need to thrive.

PART ONE: RATIONALE FOR THRIVE

- The three main inhibitors to thriving
- Social-Emotional Learning
- School improvement through focus on the "big three"

THE THREE MAIN INHIBITORS TO THRIVING

Our only limitations are those we set up in our own minds (Hill, 1937). The more time I spend working with schools, and the more I learn about psychology and neuroscience, the more I find this statement to be true. While high-performing individuals, including Napoleon Hill, understood this nearly 100 years ago, it has only been in the last decade that psychology and neuroscience have caught up. The three main inhibitors to student learning, improving and thriving are simply limitations that reside in the mind.

The three inhibitors to thriving are:
- A belief that our talents and intelligence are fixed traits
- A lack of resilience and persistence
- Poor mental health

Now for a little more about each one.

The first inhibitor – A belief that our talents and intelligence are fixed traits

This is exposed by students through a lack of belief in themselves and their ability to change and improve (or in some cases, too much belief in their natural ability).

Over the years, I have heard so many students say things like: "I'm just not good at history"; "spelling just isn't my thing"; I don't have an artistic bone in my body"; or "my mum wasn't good at maths, so that's why I'm not good at maths".

In fact, I have said things like this myself. At the important transition between primary and secondary school, like many students, I was really excited about going to high school. I was a good student, but I was worried about one elective subject that I didn't want to do – art. My beliefs were along the lines of:

"I don't have an artistic bone in my body"; "Mum was good at art, but that gene seemed to have skipped me and gone to both of my sisters"; and "I'm just not good at art."

I was okay with this because I knew and understood that we are all different and I had other "gifts". I seemed to have a "gift" for soccer, maths, music and long distance running. This brings us to the next problem.

Like many students, I believed I was naturally more gifted than others in certain areas. Because I was gifted, or blessed with these talents, I was destined for success. It didn't require me to practice my mathematics; it just seemed to come more naturally to me than to others.

Our belief system (or self-talk) may be telling us, "I'm a natural at maths" or "maths just isn't my thing". In either case, it is the manifestation of a fixed mindset. This is a mindset that is based on the notion that intelligence is static, rather than developed. It is harmful to our potential and inhibits thriving in our lives.

The antidote for this is to learn about and develop a growth mindset (Dweck, 2006). This is the belief that intelligence and talent are developed over time through effort, focus, attention and deliberate practice. It is also valuable to learn about the human brain and its potential – particularly the concept of neuroplasticity, which makes this development possible.

In order to cultivate the growth mindset, our schools and homes should be places that encourage and value effort, growth, focus, persistence, learning, improvement, deliberate practice and honest feedback. Instead, research reveals that some schools and homes reinforce the belief that some people have "it" and others don't. It is an unintended message that we communicate to our students. While the message may be innocent and unintended, it is harmful to our growth and to the growth of young people in our care. It is my mission to ensure that every school embodies the growth mindset in order to cultivate thriving in our schools. More on this in Part 2.

The second inhibitor – A lack of resilience and persistence

A lack of resilience is demonstrated by students who give up when confronted with obstacles or setbacks. A lack of persistence can be noticed in a reduction of focused effort over a period of time. Over the last couple of years, I have had the opportunity to speak with many educators from a range of schools. Through these conversations and my own anecdotal research in schools, it would seem that this is currently the most prevalent inhibitor to learning. There is a growing body of evidence to support these claims.

An example of students who lack resilience was reported to me by a high school science teacher. He explained that many students who attempted science experiments frequently gave up when it didn't work out the first time. Imagine if Thomas Edison gave up after his first few attempts – we might still be in the dark!

Another example of students who do not recognise the value of persistent, focused effort comes from a Year 11 Business Management class I taught a few years ago. Students were completing business plans which were, of necessity, quite lengthy. When I returned the marked assignments, I noticed that one of the students seemed disappointed with her results. I decided to enquire about this with her. She explained that she had put in her best effort with this assignment; however, she was disappointed with her C+ grade. I asked her what she meant by "best effort". She explained that she had spent approximately three hours on the task over the two nights before the work was due. I could recall receiving a poor draft from this particular student.

The story is probably all too familiar for many classroom teachers. So I decided to use this natural conversation as a teaching point with the rest of the class. There were two students who had received either an A or A+ in the class. I asked all of the students to estimate how many hours they had spent on this task in their own time. Their responses ranged from 3-5 hours, through 10-15 hours, all the way up to 30+ hours. No prizes for guessing which two students had put in more than 30 hours on this task! For these two students, that correlated to the level of effort they would usually contribute for a piece of assessment.

I do not mean to propose that any student who spent 30 hours or more on the task would have received an A or A+. There are other more complex factors at work. The two students who had done that for this task have demonstrated this work ethic for as long as they could remember- and other students usually call them "smart". That day however, it became clear to all the students that there was a relationship between time, energy and effort invested into study and academic outcomes. In this instance, spending three minutes articulating something that might be very obvious to me as an educator was a very valuable learning experience for my students.

While some students struggle to recognise the benefits of resilience and persistence, it seems others have the ability to stick with things when the going gets tough. Some students seem to be able to put in the hard work, with an understanding that good things take time. Many students who participate in endurance events, such as swimming, running and cycling outside school learn the value of persistent effort. Many of the top classroom learners are at the top because they apply themselves more than others. They have invested more into their studies over the years, built good habits and continued to acquire and develop their skills over time. The attributes of persistence and resilience are life skills that are transferable to other fields. The students who have learned persistence and resilience are often at the top of their cohort in just about everything they do. While many might consider them to be talented or gifted, if we delve a little deeper or look at the research, it becomes clear that those who make it are not always the most talented (Bloom, 1985).

The remedy for a lack of persistence and resilience is to learn about, and develop, grit within ourselves and the young people in our care. Grit is resilience combined with persistence, and it is a powerful predictor of achievement in any field (Duckworth, 2007). Thriving schools and families enable young people to understand grit and how it applies to their personal aspirations. More on this in Part 3.

The third inhibitor – Poor mental health

Poor wellbeing is revealed through a general lack of mental health, increased stress, anxiety and depression. Schools do not exist in a vacuum; they are a microcosm of society. Studies show that worker happiness is at an all-time low (Riggio, 2010). In a 2007 study of 13,500 university students, 94 percent felt overwhelmed by everything they had to do, and 45 percent were too depressed to function properly (Kadison, 2005). In another study of the general population, a sample of 520,000 people revealed that only 28 percent were considered to be "emotionally well-off" (Rheault & McGeeney, 2011). Our learners are on a quest for wellbeing without many suitable role models in this area.

The results of this for our young people are predictable. In a study of over 10,000 Australian school students, 40 percent were identified as having "low levels of social and emotional wellbeing", while 31 percent were stressed (Bernard, 2007).

Most educators would agree that their subjective experience is in line with the research. Many high schools state that there has been an increase in the number of students attending with complex social and mental health disorders. Primary schools, on the other hand, are noticing more mental health issues at younger ages than ever before. I have come across many students in schools who have been required to deal with much more than I would ever imagine (separation of parents, bullying, suicide in the family, substance use by a sibling and/or sexual or physical abuse). So it is easy to see why wellbeing is an area of concern.

While teachers may consider a lack of resilience and persistence to be the big inhibitors, most school counsellors I have spoken to identify poor mental health as the major issue facing schools today. This has serious implications for the "core business" of schools. Students with good mental health and wellbeing are clearly better equipped to cope with the everyday demands of school life. On the other hand, learning is inhibited for those students with poor mental health and wellbeing (Sawyer, 2000). Improving wellbeing leads to improved performance in the workplace and in the classroom. As a result, schools and organisations that want to improve results are increasingly targeting wellbeing.

Given the current levels of poor mental health in schools and in society as a whole, as educators and parents we should be encouraged to equip ourselves and our students with some skills for managing our wellbeing. Prevention is better than cure. The pressures of life and the complexity of society are not likely to desist. Therefore the hope rests with those educators and parents who will continue to seek out ways to enhance their own wellbeing and to embrace the challenge of imparting some of these skills to our young people. Positive education has been described as teaching wellbeing to young people (Seligman, 2011). Thriving schools will embrace positive education to enhance wellbeing. However, wellbeing is also an appropriate vehicle for schools to enhance the accomplishment of their students and staff. More on this in Part 4.

Summary

There are three main inhibitors to student learning, improving and thriving. Each of these has a particular antidote that can be taught by educators and parents. They can also be learned and practiced by educators, parents and students and utilised to contribute to a thriving school community.

- A belief that our talents and intelligence are fixed traits – the antidote to which is a growth mindset
- A lack of resilience and persistence – the antidote to which is grit
- Poor mental health – the antidote to which is wellbeing

If building growth mindsets, grit and wellbeing in a school setting is of interest to you, resources and lesson plans are available at: https://www.unleashingpersonalpotential.com.au/resources.html.

In order for schools to begin the journey towards thriving, we look to the research around the broader topic of social and emotional learning.

SOCIAL AND EMOTIONAL LEARNING (SEL)

"We must remember that intelligence is not enough. Intelligence plus character—that is the goal of true education"—Martin Luther King Jnr.

Social and Emotional Learning (SEL) is the process of acquiring particular skills or competencies that leads to the development of greater social and emotional wellbeing (Stafford, 2007). Although it is named SEL, the words "personal and social capability", "personal/ emotional" and "pastoral care" are used interchangeably throughout the literature and within educational organisations (ACARA, 2013). It is widely accepted that SEL encompasses self-awareness, self-management, social awareness and social management (Goleman, 2006) – terms used in the Personal and Social Capability outlined in the Australian Curriculum.

Outcomes for schools would typically result in students learning to understand themselves and others, recognising and regulating emotions, making responsible decisions, managing their relationships, lives, work and learning more effectively, developing empathy for others, establishing and building positive relationships, working effectively in teams, handling challenging situations constructively and developing leadership skills (ACARA, 2013). These valuable skills can be learned through interactions in the home and wider community. However, these skills should also be learned through explicit instruction in the school setting (Stafford, 2007).

In addition, *"The Melbourne Declaration on the Educational Goals for Young Australians* recognises that personal and social capability assists students to become successful learners, helping to improve their academic learning and enhancing their motivation to reach their full potential. [Developing] the personal and social capabilities supports students in becoming creative and confident individuals with 'a sense of self-worth, self-awareness and personal identity. [This] enables them to manage their emotional, mental, spiritual and physical wellbeing', with a sense of hope and 'optimism about their lives and the future'. On a social level, it helps students to 'form and maintain healthy relationships' and prepares them 'for their potential life roles as family, community and workforce members'" (MCEETYA, 2008).

The need for high quality SEL in schools

"In too many classrooms and schools, children are missing a critical piece of their education. Year after year, and test after test, students and their teachers focus on the cognitive elements of education, while other life skills are often absent from the in-school experience. Reading and writing are intentionally taught, but not always resilience and responsibility. Arithmetic and higher math skills are embedded in school goals, but not necessarily persistence and grit. In some classrooms, an "either/or" dynamic has been established where core knowledge is taught, but not the skills to work cooperatively with others, resolve conflicts, and persevere. The research overwhelmingly shows the linkages among SEL, student outcomes, and school performance. [Many teachers] understand that SEL promotes young people's academic success, engagement, good behaviour, cooperation with others, problem-solving abilities, health, and wellbeing, while also preventing a variety of problems such as truancy, alcohol and drug use, bullying, and violence. In recent years, we have seen many promising signs of progress." (Civic Enterprises, 2013)

But we have more work to do in this area in order to develop thriving students and school communities.

Most schools are already implementing some form of SEL program. Nearly all teachers (88 percent) say that SEL occurs in their school on some level (Civic Enterprises, 2013). However, the success of such programs varies a great deal from school to school and from classroom to classroom. While almost every educator would agree that these skills are essential for students, many would much rather be teaching content in their preferred teaching areas. However, for students to achieve in any learning area, they must first be equipped with the mindsets, attitudes and attributes that lead to high achievement.

One major challenge for educators is that not all students walk through the classroom door optimised and ready for learning in each subject. By investing time in SEL in schools, we are endowing students with the skills they need to thrive in each of their subjects. These skills are useful during their time at school, but students can also apply these skills to every area of their lives outside, and beyond, their time at school.

There is a growing body of evidence that proposes that SEL is a vital aspect of school improvement. One of the most thorough and illuminating meta-analyses of SEL was conducted for CASEL. The study included 213 different SEL programs involving 270,034 primary and high school students. The results were significant. Compared to controls, SEL participants demonstrated significantly improved social and emotional skills, attitudes, and behaviour. In addition, students who had participated in the SEL programs reflected an additional 11 percentile-point gain in achievement (Durlak, et al., 2011). Current research points to evidence that quality SEL drives learning improvement.

Further to this, leading educational researcher and consultant, Michael Fullan, made specific recommendations for Ontario's school system to move from "great to excellent"; it must focus on two areas: sustaining improvement and implementing the six Cs. The six Cs include: character education, citizenship, communication, critical thinking, collaboration and creativity (Fullan, 2013). Most of these are considered to fall into the area of SEL.

Other support from the research includes a study of an SEL program entitled the Child Development Project. The study identified improvements in students' school-related attitudes and grade point averages, compared with the control groups that did not participate in the program (Battistich, Schaps & Wilson, 2004). This is supported further by a significant body of research that links a range of SEL programs to higher academic performance and other positive outcomes (Zins, 2007; Elias, et al., 1997; Aronson, 2002). Current research suggests there is a strong correlation between SEL and performance. Schools that invest quality time in SEL gain significant benefits.

I suggest that schools can no longer underestimate the value of this area. The evidence that links SEL to improvements in behaviour, engagement, wellbeing, attitudes and academic achievement is substantial. "Schools will be most successful in their educational mission when they integrate efforts to promote children's academic, social and emotional learning" (Elias, et al., 1997). Some of the lighthouse schools in the country have adopted the approach (such as Geelong Grammar, Brisbane Grammar and Wesley College) and are thriving as a result.

Interestingly, the majority of teachers agree about the value of SEL. For example, 93 percent of teachers see SEL as fairly important or very important for the in-school student experience. 95 percent of teachers view SEL as teachable and 97 percent report that it will be helpful for students from all backgrounds and socio-economic groups. Seventy-seven percent of teachers believe that SEL will increase standardised achievement test (SAT) scores and overall academic achievement. More than three-quarters of teachers believe that SEL will be of major benefit to students because of the positive effect on workforce readiness (87 percent), life success (87 percent) and college preparation (78 percent). Of the teachers who identified with having a "negative school climate", 80 percent viewed SEL as a possible solution (Civic Enterprises, 2013). The opinion of the majority of the teaching cohort aligns closely with the evidence (Durlak, et al., 2011).

The Australian Curriculum has identified seven general capabilities. In the years prior to the release of the Australian curriculum, educators and schools seemed to focus their efforts on literacy, numeracy, ICT capabilities and at times, critical and creative thinking (these are currently four of the general capabilities). However, personal and social capability has now been identified as a general capability (ACARA, 2013). The personal and social capability is aligned with SEL, which provides further support and validation of the need for SEL in Australian schools.

It would seem that many of our schools are trying to prepare students for work in the 21st century by giving them a laptop to use like an old fashioned notebook. I don't believe using a keyboard is going to set them apart in the employment market. This is increasingly the case for "technical professionals" (Bancino & Zevalkink, 2007).

So what skills are employers really looking for in the 21st century economy? In a 2006 survey of 461 business leaders, results indicated that it is the soft skills that give people the competitive edge. "While reading, writing and arithmetic (the 3 R's) are still fundamental to every employee's ability to do the job, employers view "soft" skills as even more important to work readiness" (Are they really ready to work? Employers' perspectives on the basic knowledge and applied skills of new entrants to the 21st century US workforce, 2006). Soft skills include communication, collaboration, problem solving, initiative, personal responsibility, persistence and teamwork. Students develop these "soft" skills through an SEL focused curriculum.

Whether we value academic achievement, workforce readiness, behaviour, engagement, positive attitudes, connectedness, school culture or persistence, the evidence points to the need for being intentional about SEL in our schools. There is a huge body of literature that emphasises a requirement for SEL in our schools. However, as many school administrators and middle level leaders will attest, there remains some resistance with the implementation of SEL in the school setting.

I will outline some of the observations I have made during my time working in, and alongside, schools.

Arguments against SEL in schools

While SEL seems to have a great deal of "in principle" support from most educators, there is a slight lack of transference into the real world of school practice. I have observed a certain stigma around SEL in Australian schools. It seems to be attributed with much less value than other learning areas. Resistance to SEL seems to come in the form of the following arguments.

ARGUMENT #1 – Disagreement

Disagreement can be healthy in a school setting when all parties are informed and aware of the best currently available research. In most cases, those that disagree with the value of SEL in schools are unaware of the body of literature that highlights its significant benefits. The small percentage of teachers who disagree with implementation of SEL in schools (for a number of reasons, including that they are not aware of the research) are often outspoken about their disagreement. They put forward a number of arguments. When a person suggests we need to focus on SEL, opponents provide resistance in statements like, "I believe we need more academic rigour in this school" or "we need more time in core classes to focus on student literacy and numeracy" or "we are already struggling to get through the content".

I have also noticed that when statements like these are made in meetings, many supporters of SEL will withdraw. I have even done this myself in the past. I believe this is because many of the supporters of SEL don't have the data readily available – it is more of a suggestion that SEL helps, rather than a fact. Now, the evidence is strongly in support of SEL. If we value academic achievement, we can use SEL to improve it. We need to understand that SEL can be rigorous in and of itself.

Furthermore, by developing SEL (or personal and social capability) with our students, we can ensure that learning is more rigorous across all learning areas. By working with those who disagree (or are unfamiliar with the literature), it is possible to increase their support by sharing the evidence. Many educators are now of the belief that schools can no longer afford to avoid investing in evidence-based SEL.

ARGUMENT #2 – "There is no time"

A common argument is that there is not enough time for SEL. Eighty-one percent of teachers rank time as the biggest impediment to implementing SEL (Civic Enterprises, 2013). It is true that there is a limited amount of time for schools to work with their students. Most Australian schools are currently wrestling with the challenge of creating enough time for each of the learning areas of the Australian Curriculum. My suggestion is that it is not about cramming it all in – it is about prioritising. Research has demonstrated that SEL can increase time on task (Civic Enterprises, 2013). We need to decide what is important for the development of lifelong thriving amongst all our students.

If we want to see major gains for every student in terms of achievement, behaviour and engagement, then we will make time for SEL. It is an investment in the learning process and it gives back more quality time on task than it takes away. If we want students and school communities to thrive, we can no longer use "there is no time" as an excuse.

ARGUMENT #3 – "SEL is just about support"

All too often educators conceptualise SEL as a way to enhancing non-academic outcomes such as health, behaviour, safety, attitudes or citizenship. Although it is true that SEL improves all of these outcomes (and more), it has a critical role in improving academic outcomes (Zins, 2007). SEL enhances, rather than inhibits, the academic success of our learning communities. SEL is for achievement, not just support. Until we place value on SEL as an essential ingredient for students being able to thrive in all learning areas, we won't do it justice. Parents and educators need to be aware of the research and be very clear on the ways in which SEL has a significant positive impact on student academic achievement and beyond.

ARGUMENT #4 – Timetabling structure

For many high schools, the designated SEL/pastoral care/wellbeing lesson is the last thing scheduled in the timetable (by the Deputy in charge of creating the timetable for the school). There are many competing interests at stake here, including staffing, subjects on offer, student enrolment in each class, room availability and many other logistics. If a teacher is "under load", he or she will be required to take a SEL class.

For many teachers, SEL is the only class on their timetable they did not study at university. For example, a high school maths and science teacher might have four classes of maths and two classes of science (equating to 15–24 lessons per week, depending on the length of the lessons) and then one single period of SEL. Under these circumstances, SEL is the subject that will be given the least amount of time and attention by any teacher. This would usually mean the teacher will not facilitate the learning in these lessons at that same standard they would for their preferred learning area. The flow-on effect can result in a devaluing of this allotted time by staff and students. There is no easy solution for this. However, by educating our staff in the value and evidence supporting SEL, their attitudes towards this critical area of academic life will improve.

ARGUMENT #5 – Narrow focus

With the increasing transparency of published achievement data (for example, NAPLAN scores and QCS data), some schools have narrowed their focus. Schools are feeling the pressure to perform. In order to boost results, some will focus on improving results now by maximising time in English and Maths, to the detriment of other learning areas. This has been shown to lead to further disengagement for students and an apathy or disinterest towards learning. In his book, *The Element,* Ken Robinson states that we have "come to define intelligence far too narrowly" (Robinson & Aronica, 2009). He proposes that rather than asking, "How smart are you?" we should be asking, "How are you smart?". "There are a variety of ways to express intelligence, and no one scale could measure this" (Robinson & Aronica, 2009).

When our focus becomes too narrow, we can very quickly forget that human beings express intelligence in different ways. In saying that, improving scores on standardised achievement tests (SATs) – such as NAPLAN – would be a very good thing if it didn't come as a result of a narrow teaching and learning focus which can lead to a disengagement of learners. Schools should seek out effective ways for helping every student improve their learning and their SATs. The research is very clear: by investing time in SEL, schools will enhance their results in any standardised tests, as well as improving many other aspects of the school. It would seem to me that this is a more fruitful and ethical method for improving school achievement data.

ARGUMENT #6 – "It's not my responsibility to teach it"

In Australia, SEL is most closely aligned with the general capability, "personal and social capability". The only trouble with general capabilities is that they are often not made explicit by teachers. In high schools, in particular, it can become "someone else's job to teach that". Schools that are looking for a way forward must develop capacity within all of their teachers in the area of SEL. They need to be teachers of subjects and they also need to be committed to growing young people. Despite what many non-teachers might say, the reason most of us got into teaching wasn't really for the high pay and endless holidays (much of which is spent marking, reporting and planning to do it all again!). The reason most of us got into this "gig" was because we wanted to develop young people and be part of their journey. If that's not the motivation for anyone in education, they are in the wrong job. All teachers must increase their awareness of the value and benefits of SEL. Every educator is effectively a teacher of SEL. School principals and administrators can take up this challenge and lead all their staff on a journey of SEL. Many aspects of the school will thrive as a result – not least engagement in learning and academic achievement.

The evidence in support of SEL in schools is too substantial to ignore. It is an essential ingredient if we want our young people to thrive at school, and in their life beyond school.

SCHOOL IMPROVEMENT THROUGH FOCUS ON "THE BIG THREE"

There are pendulum swings or cycles in education. This can make it difficult to commit to moving down a particular path. Some experienced teachers become increasingly cynical of educational change, which poses challenges for administrators. While this may be challenging for school leaders, some of the questions asked by our most cynical colleagues (if they are willing to work with us) are a perfect launching pad for continuous, deep, improved learning and practice, or for casting a new vision. Cynicism alone is rarely helpful, however a spirited and rigorous discussion around some key questions before launching into something new usually is. Engaging in these discussions is also a valuable means to get the support of those that otherwise might be passive towards a new initiative. However, our conversations shouldn't just rely on opinions. Instead, they should be grounded in evidence.

When we move too quickly from one idea to another, or have too many projects on the go simultaneously, we run the risk of diluting anything of value. John Hattie's work (Hattie, 2009) on calculating the effect sizes of different techniques is valuable from this perspective. Most techniques will work to some degree, but we don't have time for everything. We need to choose the techniques that will have the greatest effect, and focus our efforts on these. This is similar to calculating a return on investment in business terms. So it makes sense that knowledgeable, professional and committed teachers would ask questions of their leaders about any new initiative.

There are great schools that do just a few things very well. There are poor schools that try to do everything well. The key is focus. Questions help us step back and think. They make us focus.

At this point, a key question is: "How can we best address the social and emotional learning needs of our school communities?"

If we are looking to implement a beneficial SEL program in our schools, some questions to ask (and consider with our staff) might include:
- What is the evidence to support the new program (or the re-focusing on the old program)?
- Is this going to be relevant?
- How is this going to enhance my teaching practice?
- Is this just another "add on", or can it be applied in an everyday way?
- How is this going to improve student learning?

It is for this reason that schools looking to improve should focus their efforts on the "big three": *growth mindsets, grit* and *wellbeing.*

They are the big three because each:
- is based on substantial scientifically validated evidence
- addresses a major inhibitor to student learning, and therefore is relevant and applicable to students
- can be applied to the lives of educators and parents as well as the lives of students, and enhance teaching practice
- can be applied in the daily interactions between educators, parents and the young people we care about, and
- has a significant, positive impact on student learning.

For students to thrive and achieve their personal best, they require a growth mindset, grit and wellbeing. This is precisely why, in order for a school community to thrive, all members must commit to the journey of developing a growth mindset, grit and wellbeing.

We will look at each one of the "big three" in turn, starting with the growth mindset.

PART TWO: GROWTH MINDSETS

- Linking growth mindsets to achievement
- Neuroscience
- The adolescent brain
- Contrasting fixed and growth mindsets
- The mindsets in action
- Mindsets at a transition point
- Praise
- Feedback in classrooms
- Implications for educators and parents

LINKING GROWTH MINDSETS TO ACHIEVEMENT

The inhibitors to thriving, (a fixed mindset, a lack of resilience and persistence, and poor mental health), all reside in the mind. It has been argued that psychological factors, or non-cognitive factors, can matter more than cognitive factors when it comes to students' academic performance. Educators, psychologists and economists have identified the importance of non-cognitive factors in achievement in both schools and the labour market (Eccles, Wigfield, & Schiefele, 2001). Non-cognitive factors include beliefs, feelings, attitudes, self-control, habits and many others. As parents and educators, you will have seen non-cognitive factors limit the young people you care about. It is also possible that you are able to identify times when non-cognitive factors have limited you as an adult.

Cultivating a growth mindset is the foundation for students being able to thrive in their learning and life. Is intelligence and talent something you are born with, or is it something that can be developed over time? The answer is not one or the other.

We are born with certain predispositions. However, much of our success has to do with our life experiences. Why does Australia usually achieve poor results on the world scale in events like skiing or ice hockey, but do well in sports like cricket and swimming? Why do Canadian kids born in the second half of the year have far less chance of ever making it as a professional ice hockey player than their peers born in the first half of the year? How can one street in England (Silverdale Road, Reading) produce more top class table tennis players than the rest of the country combined? As a society, we attribute success and accomplishments to natural talent and abilities. But this is not the whole picture. Talents and abilities are, indeed, developed over time.

Carol Dweck's research (Dweck, 2006) has identified two ways to explain achievement. First, that talent and ability are inherent (a fixed mindset). Secondly, that talent and ability are malleable (a growth mindset). The trouble with believing in the fixed mindset is that it severely limits our potential. With a fixed mindset, we believe we cannot change our innate abilities – so we don't.

The growth mindset allows us to unleash the potential we have by applying our effort and energy to develop our abilities and talents. With a growth mindset, we can take charge of how we invest our energy and effort in our lives. William James wrote that we possess enormous "amounts of resource, which only exceptional individuals push to the extremes of use" (James, 1984). The high achievers in society, and in our schools, are those who stretch their abilities further than others.

These beliefs are supported by research in the discipline of neuroscience. When students are taught that talent is malleable, their grades improve. If they are taught that intelligence and talent are developed over time, through focused effort and attention, they are able to let go of restrictive beliefs more easily and improve their academic outcomes (Good, Aronson, & Inzlicht, 2003). Fixed or growth mindsets are created through praise, feedback and stories or articles that push a particular mindset. Lessons or workshops have been found to be particularly effective for developing growth mindsets. The lessons focus on teaching students that the brain is like a muscle that gets stronger with use and that every time students work hard and learn new things, the neurons in their brains form new connections (Dweck, 2009). If we are hoping to cultivate thriving students, we will be intentional about the messages we give students.

It is important to begin by identifying connections between growth mindsets and recent findings in neuroscience.

NEUROSCIENCE

"You are today where your thoughts have brought you. You will be tomorrow where your thoughts take you."—James Lane Allen.

Neuroscience is the study of the nervous system. The following is a brief overview, intended to bridge the gap between the fields of education and neuroscience. As educators and parents, we are situated within a brain-based industry. There are some areas of neuroscience that have implications for educators, parents and students, and it is on these areas that we will now focus.

Brain development and synaptic pruning

Neurons are the basic functional unit of the brain. The human brain has approximately 100 billion neurons (Giedd, 2009). Neurons process and transmit information through chemical signals. The synapse is the connecting location between neurons, where information transmission occurs. The average human brain has roughly one quadrillion (1,000,000,000,000,000) synapses (Giedd, 2009). We have some truly amazing equipment between our ears!

In terms of brain development, almost all the neurons we need throughout our life are generated in vitro, in the first three months. The neurons then begin creating connections with many other neurons in order to find functional matches. As a result of the brain attempting to set up useful neural pathways, in the early years of life there are a lot of neural connections. This makes the brain highly inefficient. In fact, the newborn baby actually has more neural connections than their parents, or even their paediatrician! However, more neural connections at that stage do not lead to higher function.

An important part of brain development is to undergo a process called "synaptic pruning". This involves selectively eliminating the neural connections that are not useful. The purpose of pruning is to improve the efficiency of the brain by eliminating the neural connections that are not being used (Chechik, Meilijson & Ruppin, 1999). This selection process follows the "use it or lose it" principle. Synapses that are frequently used have strong connections while the rarely used synapses are weakened or eliminated (Vanderhaegen, 2010). While synaptic pruning is mostly complete by the age of sexual maturity (Iglesias, et al., 2005), there are different regions of the brain that complete this maturing process much later. More on this in the section on the adolescent brain.

Neuroplasticity

Not long ago, people in this field believed that the brain's abilities were fixed shortly after childhood. Recently, however, neuroscientists have discovered that the brain is actually malleable throughout our lives. This has opened up a new field of research called neuroplasticity. Neuroplasticity is the ability of the nervous system to make large increases in the strengths of existing neural connections and also to establish new connections (Pascual-Leone, et al., 2005). It has even been proved that adaptation to neural pathways, can occur due to behaviour, environment, neural processes, thinking, emotions, as well as changes resulting from bodily injury (Pascual-Leone, et al., 2011). It is true that our thoughts change our brain. This means that by directing our focus, attention and action towards certain areas, we strengthen appropriate neural connections. This has important implications in terms of how we are able to direct the growth of our own brains.

When the brain changes, based on the activities or experiences of an individual, this is called activity-dependent plasticity. This process allows humans to retain and form memories related to many of the functions they perform on a daily basis (Bruel-Jungerman, Davis & Laroche, 2007). For example, we remember how to drive a car each time we get in to it – the alternative would be learning how to drive it each time we need to get to work. Essentially, plasticity allows us to improve skills through practice and repetition. For example, a right-handed person may brush their teeth or write their name very poorly with his/her left hand. However, continuous practice with the less dominant hand can make both hands just as efficient. When it comes to learning a skill, repeated experiences are essential as connections become stronger and more efficient through repeated use (Nagel, 2009).

The high adaptability of the brain through the process of morphing neural connections has led neuroscientists to use the phrase "neurons that fire together, wire together". There have even been cases where people who have had a stroke that resulted in a lack of mobility and function were capable of retrieving much of their lost function by practicing and "rewiring" their brain (Doidge, 2007). In the case of a stroke, the brain functions of certain damaged areas are carried out by different areas of the brain (Kilgard, et al., 2001). The brain really is an incredible organ. Activity-dependent plasticity is responsible for changing the strength of neural connections at a synapse as a result of our experiences (Sala, Cambianica, & Rossi, 2008). Changes occur in the brain both as a result of changes in the strength of the connection between two neurons (Byrne, 1997), or through changes that occur within a single neuron (Kemenes, et al., 2006). Ultimately these processes enable us to keep learning throughout our lives. An old dog can learn new tricks after all!

THE ADOLESCENT BRAIN

Adolescence is a time of rapid transformation for a young person. While the physical changes in the body are conspicuous, "the brain's transformation is every bit as dramatic but, to the unaided eye, is visible only in terms of new and different behaviour" (Giedd, 2009). One example of this change is that an escalation of myelin occurs in adolescence as the young person prepares for increased independence. Myelin assists in the transmission of information from one neuron to another. The more myelin the faster the speed of transmission (Nagel, 2009). The process of adolescent "brain maturation allows the brain to refine itself, specialize and sharpen its functions for the specific demands of its environment" (Giedd, 2009). The process of adolescent brain development can explain some of the weird, wonderful and wacky behaviour we see from adolescents.

Do adolescents react or do they choose a response?

Essentially, our actions are determined by our brain's two duelling systems. Firstly, we have the limbic system. This is the emotional part of the brain which can cause us to react in a "knee-jerk" manner. It is a result of this "fight or flight" style limbic system that we are here today. Thousands of years ago, it was appropriate to react quickly in the face of danger to avoid harm from the environment (such as predators). It is characterised by reacting first and without thinking. The limbic system was perfectly suited to life 10,000 years ago – flooding the body with adrenaline and stress hormones and sparking a reflex reaction. This system is led by the amygdala.

The second system is the rational part of the brain. Residing mostly in the prefrontal cortex, it is responsible for thinking, drawing conclusions, planning and logic. The problems we face today usually require a little more consideration than the limbic system reaction, so instead we are often reliant on the rational part of the brain. Over the last few thousand years, the rational part of our brain has continued to evolve. Essentially, this part of our brain is the opposite of the limbic system; it allows us to think first and then respond.

While there are now two developed parts of our brain, there are times when the limbic system takes over. When we are stressed, the body produces a toxic chemical called cortisol. When our levels of cortisol are high, it only takes a small stress or pressure to trigger a stress response that might seem a little over the top, or out of character. At these times, the emotional system takes over and the brain hits its internal panic button. This response has been known as an "amygdala hijack" – and the limbic system takes over. Good choices and decision making are bypassed as we respond with our primitive limbic system. We simply react by carrying out the default option (that tends to be the only one we see at the time – such as yelling, kicking, running, disappearing, punching or swearing). Fight or flight is the result, and can lead to actions we regret later. We react (with emotions), rather than thinking and then choose a response.

Furthermore, the brain typically develops from the inside-out and from back-front. For example, the pre-frontal cortex (which is responsible for planning, reasoning, impulse control, decision making, predicting outcomes, regulating emotions and abstract thinking) is the last area to be developed in the human brain, usually well after the teenage years (Yurgelun-Todd & Killgore, 2006). This maturation occurs even later for males. While the early maturing limbic system allows the adolescent to experience emotions, their late-maturing frontal lobes are not yet optimised for regulating those emotions (Giedd, 2009). This may explain (but not excuse) some of the interesting student behaviour we see in our schools! Behaviours that are prevalent at this age would include increased novelty seeking, risk taking, a shift toward peer-based interactions, exploring new environments and seeking unrelated mates (Giedd, 2009). There is a tendency to react then think, instead of thinking then responding.

In one study, psychologist Richard Davidson researched what made some people more resilient in the face of setbacks than others. He gave participants in the study a stressful and difficult situation, while simultaneously tracking their brain activity using fMRI (functional Magnetic Resonance Imaging). He was interested particularly in monitoring their limbic system and frontal lobe activity. The study found that those who were the least resilient participants were found to have increasing activity in the limbic system. The more resilient participants had a small, fast wave of limbic system activity before the frontal lobe took over almost immediately (Goleman, 1998).

Current research asserts that the brain has great potential for growth and change throughout life – much like the muscles of our body. The brain is malleable, and adolescence is a time of high adaptability. It is capable of significant change and growth. New connections are formed every time we attempt a new activity or learn something new. Existing connections are strengthened every time we practice a skill we have already acquired, allowing us to further improve the skill. The implication here is that intelligence and talent can be developed.

Neuroplasticity has major implications for human thriving as well as student learning. A basic working knowledge of the brain and its malleability underpins the growth mindset and is essential for anyone who wants to help young people to thrive.

CONTRASTING FIXED AND GROWTH MINDSETS

"I don't divide the world into the weak and the strong, or the successes and the failures. I divide the world into the learners and the nonlearners."–Benjamin Barber.

It matters a great deal what students believe about their intelligence and talent – whether it is dynamic or static. The response to this question is aligned either to the concept of fixed mindsets or to the concept of growth mindsets. If we have a fixed mindset, we will have no reason to try to improve. Instead, if we understand a growth mindset, we will want to build and strengthen neural pathways by focusing our effort. With a growth mindset, we have a reason to apply ourselves – and this shows in the results of students who hold growth mindsets. As mindsets can be changed, it is in the best interests of parents and educators to learn and explain the mindsets to the children in our care.

"In a fixed mindset students believe their basic abilities, their intelligence, their talents, are just fixed traits. They have a certain amount and that's that, and then their goal becomes to look smart all the time and never look dumb. In a growth mindset students understand that their talents and abilities can be developed through effort, good teaching and persistence. They don't necessarily think everyone's the same or anyone can be Einstein, but they believe everyone can get smarter if they work at it." —Carol Dweck, Stanford University

This graphic gives a useful overview of the two mindsets, most of which is referenced in the literature.

Fixed Mindset		Growth Mindset
☐ Innate ☐ Unchanging	**SKILLS**	☐ Result of hard work ☐ Can always improve
☐ Something to avoid ☐ Will reveal lack of skill ☐ Overwhelm	**CHALLENGES**	☐ Embrace ☐ Opportunity to change ☐ Calls for perseverance
☐ Not necessary ☐ Linked to not being good enough	**EFFORT**	☐ Essential ☐ Leads to mastery
☐ Produces defensiveness ☐ Personalised	**FEEDBACK**	☐ Useful and positive ☐ Welcomed ☐ Identify areas to improve
☐ Blame others, not my fault ☐ Easily discouraging	**SETBACKS**	☐ Opportunities to learn from ☐ Focus on making changes

(Source: http://nextstepslcc.com/wp-content/uploads/2015/01/FixedGrowth.png)

Listen to the mindsets

For educators and parents, I suggest listening out for evidence of fixed and growth mindsets. They are usually articulated loud and clear either by ourselves or by the young people we care about. The following statements may be indicators of a fixed mindset.

- "I'm not creative."
- "I'm not good with numbers."
- "I'm just not much of an athlete."
- "I don't have an artistic bone in my body."

But also watch out for hidden messages. We think of them as over-confident or "cocky", and therefore, they may not be spoken out loud as frequently. However, the reality is they are just indicators that a young person values innate ability over effort. These statements attribute success or achievement to factors outside our control.

- "I was born smart."
- "I have a gift for story writing."
- "I am naturally good at sport."

When we start to listen out for this sort of language, it becomes easier to apply the theory of growth mindset in practical terms. In every interaction, we can foster the growth mindset. By attributing a certain level of performance to effort (or a lack thereof), we can encourage the growth mindset. We can attribute success in a particular area, not to ability or talent, but rather to the time, energy, effort and practice someone has invested in order to learn and develop their skills. This is as relevant for the family watching Friday night football, as it is to the school Principal addressing an assembly full of malleable young minds.

I have two young boys. Being aware of the growth mindset is fascinating as I watch their development. Every skill they have ever learned (sitting up, crawling, walking, riding a bike and talking) has occurred as a result of their brain's capacity to change and grow. In each case, the young human beings were not afraid of failing or looking silly. They believed they could learn anything.

Recently, my eldest son, Elijah, learned to swim under water. We were very proud of him and he was proud of himself. Being aware of the power of growth mindsets, my wife and I are always very aware of the growth-minded language we use around our kids. So, we were sure to articulate to Elijah that it was the effort we valued. We explained to him that it was through practice that he learned the new skill. The performance (swimming under water) was simply a result of the process. Despite how proud of him we are, we have made a commitment not to call our boys clever, smart, intelligent, talented, gifted, or other words that connote an innate ability for something. These things are out of his control. By the way, this view is not accepted by the grandmothers on both sides; they take great delight in having "clever" grandkids! But that's not the point. To my great delight, when Elijah got out of the water and I wrapped a towel around him, I explained once again that I was very proud of his effort and how he hadn't given up even though it was hard. The next thing he said was, "What grown-ups do, I think I can do". I was amazed. He knows he can learn anything.

Babies believe they can learn anything, and they learn to walk and talk. Three year-olds learn to count and swim underwater. But then in year 9 maths classes kids think it's okay to say, "I'm just not good at maths". In reality, they should say "I'm not good at maths…YET". The truth is their brains are malleable and they can develop their skills in any area. Prior to my son learning to swim underwater, he could have (correctly) pointed out to me that, "I'm just not good at swimming underwater". The fact that it was true at the time didn't change the fact that he did learn.

Ronald E. Osborn stated that "Unless you try to do something beyond what you have already mastered, you will never grow." If a year 9 student is not good at maths yet, they can learn. However, if they believe they can't learn, they probably won't. Further to this, even if they do hold a growth mindset, a failing maths student probably won't get an A+ this semester simply by changing their beliefs – there are other factors at play. However they will achieve much closer to their potential. They will be closer to thriving. They will be building skills that would not otherwise be built. They will be directing the growth of their brain.

Infants stretch their skills daily – they are always learning and improving. However, in studies of children as young as four, children displayed fixed mindset traits and language. In Carol Dweck's research, children with a fixed mindset chose to redo an easy jigsaw puzzle rather than attempt a harder one (Dweck, 2006). They wanted to succeed and look smart. On the other hand, the growth minded students chose one harder jigsaw after another. They wanted to stretch themselves and get smarter. At the other end of the spectrum, students at the University of Hong Kong were given the opportunity to take an English course. All of the courses, textbooks and assessment at the university were in English. During their induction at the university, researchers asked all of the students who were known to be lacking in English skills a question. "If the faculty offered a course for students who need to improve their English skills, would you take it?" They also measured their mindsets. You can probably guess the results – growth-minded students emphatically agreed that they would do the course, while their fixed-minded counterparts were not very interested (Dweck, 2006). Learning starts with a mindset. Every skill we have ever learned has been developed over time, by wiring our brain circuitry to carry out the function.

Preaching to the choir?

In my work with educators, you would hope that I am "preaching to the choir". However, I have not found this to be the case – as some educators have fixed mindsets towards certain students – believing that some students can get better and better, while others just aren't good at learning. The research shows that this has an effect on student achievement (Dweck, 2009). I do not blame teachers who hold this belief. They simply are unaware of the concept of neuroplasticity and how it can be applied to learning.

In my work with schools, I have found staff to be as fascinated by this concept as the students I work with. It seems to cause a serious paradigm shift. I am a realist. Realistic is not synonymous with pessimistic. I have spent time in schools and I have read the research. It is true that we need to be realistic with expectations about what students can achieve in a certain amount of time. As educators, we also need to manage what may be (at times) unrealistic expectations of some parents. This occurs a great deal in secondary schools at the time of the Senior Education and Training (SET) Plan, which involves students selecting subjects for their final years of school.

However, if we are committed professionals who work in a brain-based industry, we are responsible for using our knowledge of the brain's capacity to adapt, change, learn and improve to better educate students. This does not involve enrolling students in senior subjects they have failed to complete at a satisfactory level up until that time (based on the promise "next year I will work harder"). The best way I have seen schools measure improvement is through "effect sizes" – a concept popularised by John Hattie's research (Hattie, 2009). We need to understand and accept that students are at different stages of the learning journey, but simultaneously recognise that each one is capable of improvement. While they will acquire information at different rates, every student can develop new skills and move forward. The reason that certain students perform higher than others has to do with the level of deliberate practice they have invested in a particular activity. There will be more on deliberate practice in Part 3 on grit.

Many people use IQ as a way to explain why some students are not capable of learning – it seems like a reasonable argument. However, even Alfred Binet, the developer of the IQ test believed that with practice and training, we can become more intelligent than we were before. He did not develop the tests so that kids could be labelled as learners and non-learners. Instead, he believed that all students could learn. He designed the IQ test in order to identify which students required extra help in the learning process. While some philosophers asserted that an "individual's intelligence is a fixed quantity which cannot be increased", Binet argues that we "must protest and react to [this] brutal pessimism" (Binet, 1909). This has been supported 100 years later, by the present day guru of intelligence, Robert Sternberg who states that "the main constraint in achieving expertise is not some fixed prior level or capacity, but purposeful engagement" (Sternberg, 2003). Even the IQ gurus themselves have been huge advocates for what we now call the growth mindset.

THE MINDSETS IN ACTION

"Hard work beats talent when talent doesn't work hard."—Tim Notke

With a growth mindset, we are free to go about improving how smart or talented we are, through effort. While with a fixed mindset, we must prove how smart or talented we are through a lack of failure. The research indicates that a student's mindset creates an entire psychological and motivational framework that has widespread effects (Blackwell, Trzesniewski & Dweck, 2007). For example, research has found that university students with a fixed mindset will pass up important opportunities to learn if there is a danger they will do poorly or expose a deficiency (Hong, et al., 1999). This is true even if it means they are putting future achievement in jeopardy by refusing to take up such opportunities. Students with a fixed mindset are also more likely to engage in self-handicapping (Rhodewalt, 1994). They may, for example, watch television instead of studying the night before a test. Obviously, this reduces performance on the test, however it enables students to preserve their sense of their own ability if they don't perform well. I, like many teachers, have heard students after a test (almost proudly) say "I didn't even do any study for this test." In many cases, it is just another example of the fixed mindset in action – their reason for not studying is that if they were to study and still underperform, this would indicate a lack of ability. I can think of many similar examples in school sport. For example, after a strong athletic performance, students will casually explain, "I didn't even train." This clearly demonstrates that they value natural talent much higher than effort. As we will discover in the next section, deliberate practice is required for students to achieve at increasingly higher levels.

Different mindsets also create different attitudes toward effort. Those with a fixed mindset believe that effort is a sign of low intelligence (Blackwell, Trzesniewski & Dweck, 2007). Effort is seen as the enemy. They believe that if you have ability you do not require effort. The thing that will determine their level of success in the future is undervalued – leading to a lack of improvement, growth, development and achievement over time. In contrast, students with a growth mindset believe that effort is a good thing, something that helps build abilities. From this perspective, effort is the necessary ingredient for performing at our best. These different beliefs about effort play a critical role in explaining the differences in achievement between those with a fixed and those with a growth mindset.

The mindsets also influence students' reactions to setbacks. Students with a fixed mindset believe that failure demonstrates a lack of ability (Blackwell, Trzesniewski & Dweck, 2007). In conjunction with this, they display a lack of persistence. Thus, when students believe they lack a particular ability, they do not see positive options for bringing about success in that area in the future. They think to themselves, "What's the point in trying if I'm not good at it?" Students with a growth mindset believe that school failures reflect more readily on their effort and their study or learning strategies. As a result, they react to challenges and setbacks with persistence. They increase their effort and seek new learning and strategies (Dweck, 2009). They also listen to feedback and are on the lookout for new and different approaches to challenges. Views about mindset are related to whether an individual attributes success or failure to their application or their level of talent in a particular pursuit.

Locus of control

There seem to be some similarities between the recent research on mindsets and earlier theory regarding locus of control (Rotter, 1966). "A locus of control orientation is a belief about whether the outcomes of our actions are contingent on what we do (internal locus of control) or on events outside our personal control (external locus of control)" (Zimbardo, 1985). Having an external locus of control allows students to attribute success or failure to factors such as natural ability, talent, genetics and intelligence. If success is caused by factors outside our control, what's the point in trying? One of the biggest determinants of our success is the belief that our behaviour matters; that we have control over our future (Achor, 2010). With a fixed mindset, we believe that those with innate abilities will always finish above those without those abilities – as achievement resides outside the perceived locus of control. That's the trouble with the fixed mindset.

MINDSETS AT A TRANSITION POINT

There are certain stages that expose the fixed mindset within students. Typically, students find the transition to high school very difficult (Eccles, Wigfield, & Schiefele, 2001). The work gets harder and the support and care of a single core primary school teacher is distributed among a number of new secondary school teachers who generally don't see any group of students more than five to six hours per week (although some secondary schools are attempting to increase this). Some secondary school teachers have five or six different classes, so they teach as many as 180 different students each week! This can mean the teaching is less personalised. On top of this, adolescents' bodies (and brains) are transforming at a rapid rate. It is little wonder that a significant proportion of Australian students in junior secondary school experience disengagement, dips in educational attainment, declines in levels of prior learning, a lack of interest in school and underachievement. This is demonstrated by some students moving backwards on standardised test scores during this period (Pendergast, 2009). When students have been tracked over challenging school transitions, such as moving to high school, researchers have found that those with the growth mindset out-achieve those with the fixed mindset. In a study of over 400 students who were followed across the transition to high school, those students who displayed a fixed mindset showed poorer motivation, less resilience in the face of difficulty and lower academic achievement over the subsequent two years. By contrast, those who had a growth mindset demonstrated improving academic achievement over the subsequent two years (Blackwell, Trzesniewski & Dweck, 2007).

Developing a growth mindset during this transition is a critical factor in giving students maximum opportunities to thrive. It would then seem necessary for every high school to cultivate a growth mindset within their incumbent students. The research shows that such an investment will reap huge dividends.

Fixed and growth mindsets have been likened to the speedy but complacent hare, and the slow and steady tortoise. We all know that "slow and steady wins the race". However, do any of the kids in our classrooms really want to be the tortoise? I doubt it. This story could easily be misconstrued – if you are slow, dumb or lacking in a particular area, you should keep trying anyway. If everyone else falls over or falls asleep, you might be lucky enough to win (the story of Steven Bradbury's gold medal at the 2002 Winter Olympics comes to mind here). The problem with this story is that it makes talent and effort into an either/or paradigm. To achieve in life, you must either be talented or forced to work hard. The tale of the tortoise and the hare may suggest that effort is for those people who lack ability. If you have to put effort into something – school work, sport and so on – you can't be good at it. The truth is, if the hare was speedy and persistent – the tortoise would not have stood a chance in any case. Those with natural abilities in particular areas must continue to develop them. The reality is that fast and steady wins the race.

From my experience as a teacher and school administrator I observed that natural talent can lead to academic awards (even dux of the grade) and can make a student the best player on the team. That is, up until about 14 or 15 years of age. At this stage, those students who apply themselves the most are the ones who move to the top of their field, overtaking those who may have more talent. We seem to love the idea that people are "naturals" in our society – Michael Jordan, Mozart, Picasso, Rafael Nadal, Einstein and Tiger Woods. But when we learn more about their actual stories, we can see that there is much more to it than being blessed with a genetic disposition that takes them all the way to the top. Natural ability is great, but when you combine ability with effort, you have a truly powerful combination. Angela Duckworth explains that effort multiplies our talent (Duckworth, 2007). If we apply no effort to something we have talent in, it equals zero! As Binet once said, "It's not always people who start out the smartest who end up the smartest" (Binet, 1909).

PRAISE

Research has shown that when adults praise children for their intelligence or talent, as opposed to their effort, it fosters a fixed mindset (Mueller & Dweck, 1998). Unfortunately, in a 1996 study, 85 percent of the parents polled believed that praising children's ability (i.e. their intelligence or talent) when they perform well is necessary to make them feel that they are smart (Mueller & Dweck, 1996). It might make them feel smart at the time (and they love the praise), but it will actually undermine their performance and simultaneously create a fixed mindset. "Attributing children's good performance to intelligence may have an undesired impact on children's overall achievement" (Mueller & Dweck, 1998). Essentially, praising for ability can do more harm than good. You don't need to feel bad for giving this sort of praise to your children or students. However, the research recommends that you stop doing it– there is a far better alternative.

A study of 53 families over five years demonstrated that praising children's *effort*, rather than *talent*, encourages them to adopt a growth mindset—they "believe ability is malleable, attribute success to hard work, enjoy challenges, and generate strategies for improvement" (Gunderson, 2013). The longitudinal study involved researchers observing families for 90 minutes every four months in their regular home environments. The children were aged between one and three when the study began, and the final follow-up was conducted when they were aged between seven and eight years old. Children who received a greater proportion of process praise ("you worked hard") [tended] to believe that the "sources of their accomplishments are effort and deliberate practice", whereas children who heard a greater proportion of person praise ("you're so smart") [tended] to believe that the sources of their accomplishments are fixed traits" (Gunderson, 2013). This study has significant implications for every educator and parent.

It is quite simple to move towards process praise instead of person praise in our daily interactions with young people. If we supervise staff, the same applies. I have found this to be a useful, simple outline for parents and staff.

Instead of person-praise like...	Try process-praise like...
Great job! You must be smart at this.	Great job! You must have worked really hard.
You got it! I told you that you were smart.	I like the way you tried all kinds of strategies on that maths problem until you finally got it.
You are so clever.	You have learned so much because you keep working at it when it gets challenging.

Adapted from: Mueller, C., & Dweck, C. (1998). Intelligence praise can undermine motivation and performance. *Journal of Personality and Social Psychology*, 33-52.

By adjusting our praise towards the process (what is within control), we build growth mindsets, thereby encouraging persistence, effort and hard work. The result is improved performance.

In another study, researchers gave students a set of 10 moderately difficult problems from a non-verbal IQ test. When they had completed the first test, the researchers praised the students. Some were told, "Wow, you got [insert number out of 10] right. That's a really good score. You must *be smart* at this." Let's call this the **ability praised group.** Another group of students were told, "Wow, you got [insert number out of 10] right. That's a really good score. You must have *worked really hard* at this". This will be called the **effort praised group**.

And that's where it got interesting. "Both groups were exactly equal to begin with. But right after the praise, they began to differ" (Dweck, 2006). The remainder of the study involved giving all students two further sets of problems. The second set of problems was very difficult, while the third set was at the same difficulty level as the first.

After the first test, most students in the ability praised group rejected the offer to attempt a challenging new task they could learn from – they perceived this task to be threatening and seemed worried that it might expose their weaknesses. On the other hand, more than 90 percent of the effort praised group chose to tackle the challenging new task – they viewed it as an opportunity for learning and improvement. All students were given a very difficult second test and they all performed poorly. Interestingly, most of the ability praised group attributed their low scores to a lack of ability, while most of the effort praised group attributed their low scores to a lack of effort. The researchers also measured levels of task persistence and task enjoyment. They found that the effort praised group persisted longer and seemed to enjoy the new challenges more than the ability praised group. Some of them even said that the hard problems "were the most fun"! The third test was comprised of a set of 10 questions at the same difficulty as the first set. The results of the ability praised group were actually lower on the third test than on their first test (an average of 4.38). They had lost faith in their natural ability (as a result of the very difficult second test) and performed worse than when they started. The effort praised group got better (an average of 6.81). These are vastly different results for two groups that were initially aligned in terms of ability. They had used the hard problems and the teacher feedback to sharpen their skills, so that when they were given easier questions in the final test, they performed much better. The study has been replicated across ethnically, racially and economically diverse groups of students, with similar results (Dweck, 2009). It was also interesting to note that approximately 40 percent of the ability praised group lied about their results, while only 10 percent of the effort praised group lied. A single comment from researchers made all the difference.

I have summarised the findings in the table below:

The effect of praise on performance	
Test #1- Students all given the same (moderately difficult) test. After which, two groups of equal ability were formed.	
Group A- intelligence praised	Group B- effort praised
Were told, "wow, you must be really smart"	Were told, "wow, you must be really hard working"
Given option of hard or easy new tasks.	
67% chose easier option.	92% chose harder option.
Test #2- Both groups given same (difficult) test. Performance dropped for both groups.	
Test #3- Both groups given same (moderately difficult) test.	
Results declined by 20% (average of 4.38).	Results improved by 30% (average of 6.81).
40% lied about their results.	10% lied about their results.

(Dweck, 2006)

Offering the right type of praise is a powerful ingredient for thriving. The right type of praise points towards practice, effort, study, persistence, strategies, choices and work ethic. This will develop a growth mindset. For example, "I like that you kept at that hard problem until you found a solution", "Well done for challenging yourself with the more difficult novel in class", "I really value the effort that you put in during the match today", or "I noticed that you kept trying your best when your team was behind in the game during the second half". Praise like this will go a long way towards unpacking fixed mindsets and building growth mindsets. When a child (or team) doesn't win an event in sport or academics, it is a great time for learning. Instead of allowing children to decide their own reasons for being outperformed – why not propose your own mature, growth-minded reasons? Rather than good luck, maybe the other team worked harder. Rather than having more talent, the other competitors might have been training more diligently and consistently. If they were beaten by a better team, great, that's only fair. You could say, "You were beaten by a good team today. They must have been working hard. If you can train harder in future and learn from today, you should have improved next time you play them". Not only is this more honest than, "Yes, it was bad luck today, you should have won". It is also going to help them consider what they could do better next time and focus on improving. As the Dalai Lama once said, "When you lose, don't lose the lesson."

FEEDBACK IN CLASSROOMS

Growth-minded feedback can have significant positive impacts on student learning. In 2009, Hattie identified "feedback" as having a substantial effect size – meaning that it has a big impact on learning. Of the 138 different influences across 800 studies affecting 800,000 students, feedback came in at number 10. Hattie has also argued that feedback focused on the process of learning was helpful, while feedback that was an evaluation of the students' ability was not (Hattie, 2009). Since then, I have noticed that some schools are really moving forward with developing feedback into their teacher professional development plan. This is useful. However, without teaching students and teachers first about growth mindsets, feedback will not achieve the desired impact on student learning. Quality feedback makes a difference – it's about what we say. For feedback to make a positive difference, it needs to come from a growth mindset framework. If educators want to move students forward, they will be intentional about providing honest feedback that comes from the growth mindset framework.

Let us not confuse growth mindset feedback with feedback that makes kids feel good. For example, "Everyone can learn and I believe in you". Feedback from a growth mindset considers all work as work in progress. We are not reflecting on a student's ability, we are reflecting on a student's demonstration of a standard in a particular task. We separate the work from the worker and critique that work openly. In doing so, we focus on areas for improvement, further learning and developing skills at a higher level. Essentially, we are able to focus honestly on the learning and on the next steps in learning. Growth-minded feedback will enable teachers to improve the quality of the feedback they give to students.

While the quality of feedback improves when teachers are guided by a growth mindset framework, so too does the student's responsiveness to feedback. "If students know the classroom is a safe place to make mistakes, they are more likely to use feedback for learning" (William, 2011). This is supported by research at Columbia University. Participants in the study had their brain waves measured while they were asked hard questions and given feedback. The measurements tracked how interested and attentive the participants were. Those with a fixed mindset paid attention in order to determine if their answers were right or wrong. However, when the right answer was given, they paid little attention. They weren't interested in feedback focused on their improvements. On the other hand, the brain waves of those with the growth mindset showed that they paid close attention to feedback that could stretch their knowledge (Dweck, 2009).

The result of this is that in a classroom two students might get the same result – let's say a C+. The teacher approaches the students and gives them their grade and explains where they could improve. The student with the fixed mindset waits to hear what grade they got and then switches off – he or she is interested only in who got a worse result than a C+. Alternatively, the student who holds a growth mindset remains attentive and may even ask questions in order to understand how they could improve their work to ensure they get better than a C+ next time. If you are a classroom teacher, you may have seen similar responses from students in your own classes. Some students seem far more receptive to feedback than others when assignment drafts are handed back and discussed. However, all students will be more open to feedback when they are first taught about a growth mindset.

The quality of feedback will improve if teachers adopt a growth mindset framework. At the same time, the responsiveness of students to feedback will improve if they have been taught the growth mindset.

IMPLICATIONS FOR EDUCATORS AND PARENTS

#1 – Train students

Make a choice to explicitly train students in the growth mindset. Offer a structured and sequential plan for learning that serves as a platform for all learning, improvement and achievement. Schools that choose to facilitate lessons or workshops about growth mindsets can change students' mindsets. A number of studies confirm that teaching students a growth mindset leads to significant increases in their motivation to learn, their grades and their achievement test scores (Good, Aronson, & Inzlicht, 2003; Blackwell, Trzesniewski & Dweck, 2007; Aronson, Fried & Good, 2002).

#2 – Be explicit

Be very clear, intentional and explicit about where achievement derives. Is it an innate ability that makes someone a "freak of nature"? Or is it a level of effort, application or persistence that has resulted in superior skill development? If we praise for talent or ability in the school context, it leads to the disengagement of those who do not seem to possess that natural "gift". It can disengage almost every member of a student assembly if students are praised for their talent and ability. Alternatively, the same situation can provide an opportunity to teach every member of the school community about the growth mindset. A 30-minute assembly for 500 students equates to 15,000 minutes (250 hours) of learning time. If we do not use such opportunities to teach students about what our school values, we are probably wasting time. Making the most of these learning opportunities will help your students and your school community to thrive.

The following is an example of how we can be explicit in our own attribution of achievement, to build a growth mindset. They are two contrasting approaches to announcing a student's high distinction in the UNSW Science Competition.

Approach a: *"Please put your hands together for Caleb Hoover who has achieved a great result."*

Lesson: This approach does not clarify how the results were achieved. Many students will attribute the success to Caleb's natural gifts in science. Others may believe he is hard working. The truth is we have wasted an opportunity to teach students the underpinning values and beliefs that will help each of them to thrive. In front of our whole school we have turned a valuable lesson into an administrative task: handing out an award. Not only does this make for boring assemblies (except for Caleb, who received the award), it disengages the entire community. Don't forget that when the music awards are given out, students like Caleb Hoover are sitting thinking, "I could never be good at music. Lucky I have a gift for science." They could learn the growth mindset if we instead attribute their achievement to the level of time, energy and effort they have invested into it.

Approach b: *"At this school, we value growth, learning and improvement through effort, persistence and resilience. It is a result of hard work and commitment to his studies that Caleb Hoover has achieved this high distinction."*

Lesson: In this situation, we have used a student's success as a teaching tool for the whole community. We have made a statement about what we value at the school and made the achievement accessible to other students. Students can now attribute the award to Caleb's effort, rather than to his innate ability.

Another example would be using an extra-curricular performance to cultivate the growth mindset. For example, "The swimming team have consistently done the hard work. They get up before dawn to practice every day in order to develop their strength, technique and endurance. We can all learn something from their effort and we wish them all the best for their competition this weekend." Rather than, "Good luck to our swimmers who are competing this weekend".

There are numerous opportunities at school assemblies to cultivate the "big three" factors for students to be able to thrive. There is a simple way to develop a growth mindset within our learners or children. Focus on the process that leads to the achievement (effort, energy, commitment, work ethic, creativity or persistence) rather than on the attributes that lead to the achievement (talent, gift, intelligence or genetics). Words like clever, natural, gifted, talented, smart, bright and genius are counterproductive when you are trying to develop students who thrive. Don't waste these learning opportunities.

#3 – Look for the everyday applications

These are messages that can be readily incorporated into everyday classroom practices without altering the curriculum and without too much additional time and effort on the part of teachers (Dweck, 2009). They can also be incorporated in family discussions in the car, on the way back from a sporting event or practice, or at the beginning or end of a school day. Conversations at the dinner table could be started with a question that focuses on learning, improvement and effort. Carol Dweck offers some suggestions:

- What did you learn today?
- What mistake did you make today that you have learned from?
- What did you try hard at today? (Dweck, 2006)

The questions focus on effort, learning, improvement and the process, rather than the results. Be sure to participate in the discussion and share your own efforts, strategies, setbacks and learning. Doing so will attune children to value effort, and adopt a growth mindset more easily. Essentially, they will attribute their results and performance more to their level of effort, time on task, and commitment than they will to natural ability. When young people do this, they learn about realistic and practical means to improving performance and become more willing to apply themselves.

#4 – Self-fulfilling prophecy

A study in Germany by Falko Rheinberg found that when educators are growth minded their students progress. On the contrary, "when the educators have a fixed mindset, the students who entered the class underachieving, left as under achievers (Dweck, 2009). It is a self-fulfilling prophecy whereby if we believe that students cannot improve, they probably won't. The fact is that our beliefs have an enormous influence on our students and their achievement (Diehl, 2010). Imagine if growth mindsets were held by all teachers in a school. The impact on student learning over a number of years would be substantial. The whole school culture would strive to improve – kids and adults would thrive. The process starts by educating our staff about the relationship between growth mindsets and achievement in every area of life.

#5 – High challenge and high support

In 1986, Larry Daloz proposed that a model of high challenge and high support had transformative power for teachers (Daloz, 1986). Carol Dweck's work on the growth mindset supports this. Firstly, high expectations are important (high challenge), because low expectations lead to "poorly educated students who feel entitled to easy work and lavish praise" (Dweck, 2006). Teachers with a growth mindset can have high expectations with respect to the notion that if we don't work hard, we shouldn't expect great results.

Success must be earned. There are no shortcuts. If we have the best interests of young people at heart, I believe we can very clearly articulate this to them. However, strong challenges without strong support don't lead to the growth of young people. Without a supportive environment, any amount of expectation, challenge or advice will be seen as threatening. It is one thing to know that you are right in having high expectations. It is another for young people to understand that the reason we have high expectations is because we care and want to support them. The best teachers are those who foster nurturing relationships with students that feature high standards, clear expectations, honest feedback and high support. They are relationships based in the growth mindset. Honesty is essential because this allows us to give real feedback to students about their progress. This feedback can provide students with practical ways of working towards the high standards set. A growth mindset, frames this in a way that gives the learner the tools and mindset to unleash his/her potential.

#6 – Avoid the use of "dirty" words

"You learned that so quickly – you're so smart." "Wow, you're a natural at this sport". Many parents praise brains and talent, as they believe it will give their children permanent confidence. However, findings from the research quite clearly show that "praising children's intelligence and talent harms their motivation and it harms their performance" (Dweck, 2006). Other "dirty" words are clever, gifted, talented and bright – they diminish the potential of kids by cultivating the fixed mindset. If success means they are smart or talented, then failure must mean they are dumb or lack talent. Yet failure occurs when we seek to grow. When we stretch ourselves beyond our comfort zones, we can sometimes fall short. If we are afraid to fail, we will be too scared to stretch. As a result, we inhibit our own growth. John Maxwell said, "If you aren't making any mistakes, it's a sure sign you're playing it too safe". If parents and teachers want to help students thrive, they should teach their children to "love challenges, be intrigued by mistakes, enjoy effort and keep on learning" (Dweck, 2006).

It is clear to see why cultivating a growth mindset in staff and students is the first ingredient to thriving.

If building growth mindsets in a school setting is of interest to you, resources and lesson plans are available at: http://www.unleashingpersonalpotential.com.au/

PART THREE: GRIT

- Linking grit to achievement
- Failure and success stories
- Delayed gratification
- Continuous improvement
- Mastery through deliberate practice
- Goal setting
- Habit formation
- Effort and energy management

"The only thing that I see that is distinctly different about me is I'm not afraid to die on a treadmill. I will not be outworked, period. You might have more talent than me, you might be smarter than me, you might be sexier than me, you might be all of those things — you got it on me in nine categories. But if we get on the treadmill together, there's two things: You're getting off first, or I'm going to die. It's really that simple..." —Will Smith

LINKING GRIT TO ACHIEVEMENT

"When the going gets tough, the tough get going."—Joseph Kennedy

The second main inhibitor to thriving, you will recall, is a lack of persistence and resilience. Angela Duckworth is a prominent researcher in the field of grit. She defines it as "perseverance and passion for long-term goals" (Duckworth, 2007). Grit is about determination, resolve, resilience, discipline, self-control, persistence and a willingness to do whatever it takes to achieve important goals. It is a combination of resilience and persistence. People who are gritty are more resilient in the face of adversity, they bounce back after failure and disappointment, and they persist when progress is slow, boring, tedious or difficult. Grit is a factor of both nature and nurture. We are all born different so some of us may have a predisposition to certain character strengths – of which grit is one. But, like the growth mindset, character strengths can be grown or diminished, based on our actions, thoughts, choices and life experience. Grit is an action, whereas the growth mindset is an understanding. Grit is the action that leads to learning, improving and thriving. A powerful combination.

If success and achievement stem from genetics – we might as well stop teaching children about persistence, resilience and the like. However, as educators, we have all encountered latent potential in the children we teach. We have seen it dormant inside them or wasted altogether. If only they could direct their energy, attention and effort into something that would help them learn, improve, or grow then their future might be different. Grit is the key to action that unlocks human potential in every endeavour. So let's get serious about equipping every kid in every school with grit.

Grit does not simply require believing or wanting to achieve something. This is just the start of the process. A belief system and motivation are necessary but are not sufficient for the achievement of goals. Grit involves sticking with commitments until they come to fruition. It is not just about setting goals, it is about doing the things that will lead to their achievement. Grit is not about having good intentions or starting an activity – anyone can do that. Grit is about sticking with it until it is complete. Gritty individuals are distinguished by their propensity to maintain "effort and interest over years despite failure, adversity and plateaus in progress" (Duckworth, 2007).

Grit is one of the best predictors of our success in work, life and in learning. This section will investigate some of the research about grit, offer explanations as to why gritty people achieve more and how grit can be developed. Specific skills sets that contribute to grit are: delayed gratification, continuous improvement, mastery through deliberate practice, goal setting, habit formation and finally effort and energy management. Schools that foster grit will set their parents, staff and students up to thrive. As educators, we are in the field of unleashing potential. This can only happen when grit is developed.

Grit research

In a study conducted by Duckworth at West Point Military Academy it was discovered that gritty army cadets are less likely to drop out (Duckworth, 2013). West Point is an exclusive institution, reserved for the top army cadets in the USA. Students at West Point must study at the university, attend to military duties and participate in competitive athletics. Approximately 1300 cadets join West Point each year. Their first experience is a gruelling three-month summer training, known as "Beast Barracks". It is known for its intensity and as a result many cadets do not complete it and drop out before three months has passed. In this research, grit predicted retention better than any other measures such as SAT scores, class rank, demonstrated leadership ability or physical aptitude. Even when the army combined these other measures into an overall index of talent called the Whole Candidate Score, grit was a better predictor of the cadets that would make it through the summer.

In another study, Duckworth and her colleagues used grit to predict achievement at a national spelling bee (Duckworth, 2007). All the kids had natural ability, but who would win a competition with the smartest minds in the country? Duckworth supposed that it would be the gritty kids who would win. The researchers measured the levels of grit, self-control, verbal IQ and age of participants. When they controlled for age (that is, same age participants), they found that grit was a better predictor of which students would make the final round than self-control or verbal IQ. The gritty students had done more practice and had been prepared to tackle the hardest and least pleasurable problems. It is interesting to note the similarities, and the apparent correlation, between those with grit and those with growth mindsets in Carol Dweck's studies.

Why do gritty people achieve more?

If grit is a consistent predictor of success, are those lucky enough to have it destined for success? The short answer is absolutely not. The reasons that gritty people achieve more in just about every area of life can be found in the actions they would usually take in a situation. An online grit survey asks for responses to statements such as, "I have overcome setbacks to conquer an important challenge", "I finish whatever I begin", and reversed scored statements like, "My interests change from year to year" and "I have difficulty maintaining my focus on projects that take more than a few months to complete." It is a self-report survey whereby items are rated on a 5-point scale from "1–not at all like me" to "5–very much like me". You can go online and take the grit test for yourself. The key to being gritty is not getting a good score on the test. It is about actually *being* gritty. Gritty people behave differently, which explains their success. Here's another example from the research to further illustrate the point.

In two separate longitudinal studies of over 300 year 8 students, researchers found that self-discipline was a better predictor of academic success than IQ (Duckworth, 2005). Self-control was also a better predictor of improvement in test scores during 7 months of the study. Once again, it was found that those who were more self-disciplined behaved differently. It wasn't just a question of being born self-disciplined; it was a question of doing things differently. When compared to their more impulsive peers, the highly self-disciplined students "had fewer school absences, spent more time on their homework, watched less television, and started their homework earlier in the day" (Duckworth, 2005). No wonder their test scores showed significant improvement!

"Achievement is the product of talent and effort, the latter a function of the intensity, direction, and duration of one's exertions toward a goal. Whereas the amount of energy one invests in a particular task at a given moment in time is readily apparent both to oneself and to others, the consistency of one's long-term goals and the stamina with which one pursues those goals over years may be less obvious. Similarly, whereas the importance of working harder is easily [comprehended], the importance of working longer without switching objectives may be less perceptible" (Duckworth, 2007).

A combination of intensity of effort and consistency of effort over a long period of time leads to exceptional achievement. Students currently at the top of our classes are not there because they worked hard at the assignment this term; they are there because they have applied this work ethic over a number of years. This also explains why some students can "coast" for a little while. They are at the top thanks to their previous efforts and by skills they previously acquired – not by skills they were born with. This is typically what makes other students believe that these "coasting" students have a gift for a particular area.

In a 1985 study of 3,500 students from nine different universities, "follow-through" was a better predictor "than all other variables, including SAT scores and high school rank, of whether a student would achieve a leadership position in college. The follow-through rating involved evidence of purposeful, continuous commitment to certain types of activities versus sporadic efforts in diverse areas" (Willingham, 1985). "Follow-through" in this context involves perseverance and sticking with long-term goals and captures the essence of grit. This will be explained in more detail in the section on mastery and deliberate practice.

Prodigious talent and grit seem to have no correlation, or even an inverse correlation. This suggests that on average, talented people are slightly less gritty. The combination of high talent and high grit is very rare. One possible explanation for this is that highly talented individuals have had less opportunity to develop a resilient approach to failure and setbacks, due to their success (Duckworth, 2013). From this perspective, it may be better for students to finish second or third and continue to work at developing their skills, than to be top of the class at an early age.

How can grit be developed?

Grit can be developed through explicit and implicit avenues. It needs to be taught if we want to foster it in our students. However there are many ways to teach it. There are certain explicit, teachable elements of grit, for example: delayed gratification, continuous improvement, mastery through deliberate practice, goal setting, habit formation and finally effort and energy management. These topics will be covered in detail in the sections that follow. Another grit builder is providing students with real-life examples of people who have exhibited significant grit in order to achieve certain accomplishments.

It's about a creating a culture that promotes grit. Schools and families can make grit something that is valued. Share stories about how grit has paid off for you and how it contributes to the success of others at school, work, sport and in life. Conversations can come from a framework of grit development, which is not far removed from a growth-minded dinner or car conversation mentioned previously. Schools and families should eradicate the use of terms that devalue grit and instead, adopt the language of the growth mindset. Terms like work ethic, persistence, bounce back, discipline, self-control, resilience, "hard yakka" and others will let grit flourish, and as a result, people will thrive and continue to improve.

Now we turn to some of the key topics that can enhance the development of grit for young people.

FAILURE AND SUCCESS STORIES

"Many of life's failures are people who did not realise how close they were to success when they gave up."—Thomas Edison

"Only those who dare to fail greatly can ever achieve greatly."—Robert F Kennedy

Over the last couple of years, I have asked kids to come up with a model based on the words failure, success, me and then two arrows. I then ask someone from each group to explain their models. They have only ever come up with three models, as follows.

1. Failure ⬅ Me ➡ Success

The explanation for this model usually centres on the idea that our failure or success is based on the choices we make as individuals. It involves taking responsibility for choices, and in this sense the model has a good deal of merit.

2. Failure ➡ Me ➡ Success

The explanation for this model usually centres on the idea of self-improvement. The thinking is, "Today is a new day. I am making some choices now that mean that I am moving forward and improving." This is nice, but idealistic and a far stretch from reality.

3. Me ➡ Failure ➡ Success

I believe this is the best of the three models. With this model, students explain that they have their eyes fixed on success, but that there will be failure, setbacks and obstacles along the way. They have learned that they will need grit to keep moving on their journey.

If we don't acknowledge that there will be failure (or setbacks) on the journey, we create a fear of failure. By ignoring the reality of setbacks and failure, children will give up when obstacles do arise. The best way to approach this is through a process referred to as "mental contrasting", which will be discussed in the section on goal setting. Failure is a stepping stone on the road to success and the obstacles and setbacks that come along are inevitable. They stretch us and make us grow. Shawn Achor believes that we need to reject the belief that every failure will lead to more failure. In doing so we give ourselves the greatest power possible: the "ability to move up not despite the setbacks, but because of them" (Achor, 2010). We need to teach children to lean into the discomfort. Rosabeth Moss Kanter once said, "Everything looks like a failure in the middle". We have to keep moving and growing and grit helps us do this when confronted by adversity.

Some psychologists even suggest that we should fail early and often, in order to learn. While post-traumatic stress is very real, and well documented, psychologists have also noticed an unusual phenomenon – they have called it post-traumatic growth. Researchers have found that after the 2004 train bombings in Madrid, many residents experienced positive psychological growth (Val & Linley, 2006). Similar positive personal or psychological growth has been observed in people experiencing trauma and in women diagnosed with breast cancer (Weiss, 2002). While this is not the situation for every individual, researchers have found that many people are able to use adversity to "bounce forward" (Walsh, 2002). Consider this quote from Michael Jordan: "I've failed over and over again in my life – and that is why I succeed." He doesn't say, "I have failed over and over again in my life – but I press on and succeed anyway." He attributes his success to failure along the way. He has grown and improved as a result of his failure, not despite it.

After sharing these models, I believe it is worthwhile to share stories to illustrate the point to students, based on people who have had their share of setbacks. Young people seem to be intrigued by these stories; they connect to them and remember them. They are good investments into the "grit accounts" of students.

An author

In 1990, a 25-year-old woman conceived an idea for a book on a train that was delayed between Manchester and London. Writing the book consumed her and for the next few years she tirelessly worked on it in coffee shops and in her rented apartment. During this time she lived on state benefits, she experienced the death of her mother, divorce from her husband and the birth of her daughter. She was depressed and contemplated suicide. In 1995 the book was finished and it was time for publication.

The book was submitted to 12 publishing houses and each of them rejected it. A year later, a publishing house paid her £1,500 and agreed to publish the book. It was 1997 by the time the first print run of 1,000 books was complete. The book was the first in the *Harry Potter* series by J.K. Rowling. The books in this series have now sold over 400 million copies and are the bestselling book series in history. It took eight years of dedicated persistence and for J.K. Rowling to go from a "jobless failure" to the United Kingdom's bestselling author (J.K. Rowling, 2015).

An entrepreneur

In 1955, after selling his restaurant due to a new highway that diverted customers from his business, Colonel Sanders lived on $105 a month from social security. All he had was a car and a recipe for chicken. He decided he would travel around the United States offering free samples of his product and inviting restaurant owners to consider a franchise model using his chicken recipe. Apparently, Sanders visited 1008 restaurants before one restaurant owner finally agreed (reachout.com, 2014). From these humble beginnings, and through a great deal of failure, Kentucky Fried Chicken was born – it is now the world's second largest restaurant chain.

An athlete

When the 1960 Olympic games was televised internationally, a 20-year-old American woman, Wilma Rudolph became an international star. Rudolph won gold medals in the 100m, 200m and 4x100m relay (which included a world record in the 200m event). She was named as "the fastest woman on earth", "the black gazelle" and "the tornado". What many people did not know was that she had not been like this her whole life. She did, however, have an incredible work ethic. Rudolph was born prematurely at 4.5 pounds (2.0kg). She had 21 other siblings. At the age of four, she nearly died from the polio virus but suffered infantile paralysis as a result. She was left with a twisted leg and had to wear a leg brace. Over the next eight years, she vigorously pursued physical therapy. By the age of nine she was able to replace the leg brace with an orthopaedic shoe, which she wore for the next three years. The physical therapy had helped her develop strength and mobility to the point of normal function. After eight more years of dedicated training and commitment (with other children and then with other elite athletes), she would be called "the tornado". There is now an award in her name presented each year to an American athlete who faces challenges, overcomes them and strives for success (Wilma Rudolph, 2015). The award is not for talent; it is an explicit recognition of overcoming adversity.

Some other famous failures

Oprah Winfrey was fired from her first TV job after being told she was "unsuitable for television". She went on to become a billionaire with her own television talk show. She is one of the most influential people of the 21st century. The words of Captain James R Cook exemplify Oprah's story: "*Do* just *once* what others say you can't *do*, and you *will* never pay attention to their limitations again."

The Beatles were told that "guitar music is on its way out." This would have been a huge stumbling block and cause for concern for the rock band that has been considered the greatest and most influential act of the rock era. Given this feedback from so-called experts, many others may have walked away from their passion and love of music. Instead, the Beatles persisted.

The level of grit applied by all these people led them up the long and hilly terrain of success. We need to share these stories with the children we care about. If they hear about people who have lived a life filled with grit they will sense hope in the opportunities that lie ahead. They must learn that failure can lead to success. This will make a deposit into their grit account.

DELAYED GRATIFICATION

"We must all suffer from one of two pains: the pain of discipline, or the pain of regret."—Jim Rohn

In our reality TV culture, there are some misleading messages for students currently in our school system. Houses are renovated in one month, bodies are transformed in two months, and the super nanny can fix any kid (or parent) with just one three-minute visit. Powerball's catch cry, "One ball could change it all" paints the picture that in just one moment, everything can change for a person. It is easy to see why students want a quick fix in their own lives too. However, what the TV doesn't show is the far less "sexy" or marketable side. While some people, who make rapid transformations are able to maintain those positive life changes, many end up where they started. Kids implicitly learn from the media that they can get results now and they buy into the very seductive lie of instant gratification.

A study led by psychologist Walter Mischel at Stanford University in 1970 identified when the ability to delay gratification develops in children (Mischel & Ebeensen, 1970). The initial experiment involved 92 students aged between three and five years old. The researchers placed a marshmallow, pretzel or cookie on a table in the middle of a room. They explained the conditions to the children and left the room. The children were allowed to eat the marshmallow, but if they could wait for fifteen minutes for the researchers to return they would be rewarded with a second marshmallow. Of the children involved in the first study, a minority ate the marshmallow immediately. Of those who attempted to wait, one third delayed gratification and got the second marshmallow. In the initial experiment, findings were that age had a corresponding relationship with a child's ability to delay gratification. Recent research in the field of neuroscience about the developing pre-frontal cortex, as discussed earlier, explain why this is the case. There were additional studies that involved the same test under differing conditions. For example, thinking about the rewards or making rewards more prominent during the experiment both had the effect of reducing the voluntary delay (Mischel, Ebbensen & Raskoffe, 1972). However, the most interesting findings were largely unexpected and came about many years later.

The first follow-up study on delayed gratification with the same participants occurred in 1988. Mischel found that "preschool children who delayed gratification longer in the self-imposed delay paradigm, were described by their parents (years later) as adolescents who were significantly more competent" (Mischel, Shoda & Rodriguez, 1989). Another follow-up study in 1990 showed that the propensity to delay gratification was positively correlated with SAT scores, educational attainment and good health, while being inversely related to rates of crime and substance abuse (Shoda, Mischel & Peake, 1990). It is clear that those who could resist the short term temptation were much better off later in life on a large number of measures.

Another finding from an even earlier study may have more significance now, than at any other time in history. In 1958, Mischel sought to identify differences between groups of different ethnicity (Mischel, 1958). He studied a small group of seven to nine year olds from Trinidad in order to determine differences between the Indian born versus the African born children. The children were required to indicate a choice between receiving a 1¢ candy immediately or having a 10¢ candy in one week's time. Although there were differences between the age of participants, the ethnicity and the socioeconomic groups, the best predictor in the ability to delay gratification was the absence, or presence, of a father. The study showed that children from "intact" families demonstrated a superior ability to delay gratification. With so many students in our schools coming from homes where abuse is experienced, or single-parent homes, it is not surprising that educators see children struggle with delaying gratification.

There is another cultural factor that affects this issue. Twenty years ago we would post a letter. We waited quite some time to receive a response, or even to know that the letter reached its destination. Today, for young people, emails have become the new "snail mail". Instead, they prefer to Facebook message or text each other to elicit a quick response. Our children operate at "twitch-speed" and are not used to having to wait. This means that many of them devalue hard work, persistence, effort and things that take time, and prefer quick responses, quick solutions and "right now" results. But we can help them learn!

Why is delaying gratification such a powerful predictor of success later in life?

Below are some examples of how it works.

If students can delay the gratification of:
- watching television and get their homework done now, then they'll learn more and get better grades.
- buying desserts and chips at the shop, then they'll eat healthier when they get home.
- finishing their workout early and doing an extra lap of the block, then they'll get fitter and healthier. (Clear, 2014)

If eating a fast food burger caused us to drop dead after one bite, it would be easy to resist. But that's not how it works. The reason that delaying gratification is difficult is because we don't experience the pay-off immediately. If working on an assignment for two hours was going to give our students a VHA, most of them would probably do it. But the price of success is higher. If we want our kids to be grittier, we must teach them delayed gratification.

Are kids born with the ability to delay gratification?

Delayed gratification can be either developed or dissolved depending on what we learn and experience. Recently, in research conducted at the University of Rochester, researchers put a twist on the marshmallow experiment by deliberately breaking promises with some of the participants (Kidd, Palmeri & Aslin, 2013). Before the test began, they promised the children either stickers or crayons. They did not deliver on the promise for some of the students and for others (the control group) they did. Children in the control group were prepared to wait for an average of 12 minutes, while those who had had their promises broken waited for an average of three minutes. Children in the control group had learned that they could rely on the adults and also that "good things come to those who wait". Those who were in the environment of broken promises figured they were best to take the marshmallow while they could. I believe the students in our schools are much the same. If they can trust the security of their environment, they are more willing to delay gratification.

How can we build a child's ability to delay gratification?

"Success in nearly every field requires you to ignore doing something easier (delaying gratification) in favour of doing something harder" (Clear, 2014).

1. Be consistent and reliable. Follow through on promises so that children feel they can trust the environment they are in. As teachers, educators and parents we should do everything we can to assure a consistent, reliable environment for our young people.

2. Teach coping skills. There are certain things that help young people cope better. For example, in one version of the marshmallow study, participants who were successful at delaying gratification chose to ignore the marshmallow, move around the room, sing, talk to themselves or try to sleep. Those who wanted to lick or sniff the marshmallows were the least successful (although it is hilarious watching them try to resist – check out Igniter Media's re-take of it online). Simply put, those who struggled didn't have any skills to cope with the challenge. (Once upon my time, 2015).

3. Start with small wins. When opportunities arise in which to demonstrate delayed gratification, success strengthens those pathways in the brain associated with self-control. Give children opportunities to say "no" to something now, and "yes" to something more enticing in the future. It is about changing the beliefs of young people. The idea is for them to have the conviction that "when I wait for something that is promised to be better, I can trust that it will happen and that it actually is better". And secondly, "I am capable of saying 'no' to something now, in order to say 'yes' to something later on".

4. Be aware of, and use, the "hidden zero effect". Decision makers commonly view situations of delayed gratification as a choice between a good alternative now and a better alternative later. Researchers at Penn and Stanford have found there is more to delayed gratification than that (Magan, Dweck & Gross, 2008). They compared results in the hidden zero group with the explicit zero group. Those in the hidden zero group were asked, "Would you prefer $5 right now or $6.20 in 26 days?" Those in the explicit zero test were asked, "Would you prefer $5.00

today and $0 in 26 days or $0 today and $6.20 in 26 days?" Even though the choices are really variations of the same thing, the subjects in the explicit zero group showed significantly lower impulsiveness. When they were made explicitly aware of the opportunity cost (they were choosing $0 at one point or the other), they found it much easier to choose the later, better alternative. When giving kids options, and trying to develop the ability to delay gratification, it might be helpful to consider being explicit about the opportunity cost.

CONTINUOUS IMPROVEMENT

"You have to apply yourself each day to becoming a little better. By applying yourself to the task of becoming a little better each and every day over a period of time, you will become a lot better."—John Wooden.

Continuous improvement, or "kaizen", involves a focus on tiny, incremental changes over a period of time. These tiny incremental changes eventually have significant impacts. "Kaizen" took car manufacturer Toyota, and the Japanese car industry, from having a very poor global reputation, to being one of the world's leading car manufacturers over a period of ten years. They did this by making tiny improvements in work efficiency, such as moving a bin on a production line by one metre. It has been said that Toyota engineers collectively come up with approximately 1,000,000 tiny improvements to the car manufacturing process every year. This section on continuous improvement involves understanding and applying three principles that make a big difference in a person's life. These are: the slight edge, the compound effect and the aggregation of marginal gains. Each will be explained in turn, however, there is a synergy that exists between them.

The slight edge

In Jeff Olsen's book, The Slight Edge, he states, in "life or work or play, the difference between winning and losing, the gap that separates success and failure, is so slight, so subtle, that most never see it. As you walk your path, it is always, every moment of every day, curving either upward or downward."

No one notices many of the choices you make today. They don't seem to have any consequences to our lives in the long run. Whether I do some exercise or not, whether I eat something healthy or unhealthy, or whether I spend time with a loved one or not. In isolation these choices don't make much of a difference. However, they lead us on a path that Olsen refers to as the upward or downward curve. Every moment of every day, we are subject to the compound effect. The small choices on the upward curve do add up due to the compound effect.

The compound effect

"Success is a few simple disciplines, practised every day; while failure is simply a few errors in judgment, repeated every day."—Jim Rohn

The compound effect is a book that was written by Darren Hardy in 2011. In it, he gives a great example of three friends to illustrate how the compound effect works in our lives. This is a summary of each of their stories.

Larry plods along doing as he has always done.

Scott decides to make some small, seemingly inconsequential positive changes. He begins reading ten pages a day and listening to self-improvement audios. He cuts 125 calories out of each day by trading a can of soft drink for water and starts walking an extra couple of thousand steps a day.

Brad makes a few poor choices. He invests in a big screen TV so he can enjoy more of his favourite shows. He starts eating dessert more often and puts a new bar in his family room which leads him to add about one more drink per week. Nothing crazy, Brad's just looking for a little more fun.

Ten months later – no perceivable difference is seen. But fast track to twenty-five months and we start seeing measurable, visible differences. At month twenty-seven, we see an expansive difference. And, by month thirty-one, the change is startling. Brad is now overweight while Scott is trim. After investing one thousand hours reading good books and listening to self-improvement audios, Scott earned a promotion at work and his marriage is thriving. Brad on the other hand, got sluggish from the weight gain, started feeling worse about himself and retreated from his wife, which led to a marital breakdown. Larry on the other hand, is exactly where he was two years ago, but is now bitter about it.

You get the picture. The small habits we create lead to huge compounding effects." (Donahue, n.d.) The main theme of the book is that it is the small, positive, consistent actions that make a significant and lasting difference in our lives. It is not about trying to lose 10 kilograms before the start of summer. It is about changing our daily actions in order to live the life we want to live. It is about using the laws of the slight edge and the compound effect for us, rather than against us. I provide a further example to illustrate this.

Compound interest is a wonderful means of teaching delayed gratification. I take great joy in posing the question to students: would you rather $1,000,000 today, or have 5 cents today, 10 cents tomorrow, and I will continue doubling the amount given for one month? Despite their curiosity and suspicion, most students raise their hand for the million dollars now (some of them even say they will have more than a million at the end of the month because it will earn interest). I then go through the results with them at different junctures during the hypothetical month, noting the amounts over a few different days. For example, on day 8, the "5 cents doubled" group have $12.75 in the account, on day 18 they have $13,107.15 and on day 25 the total is $1.6 million. By day 30 the five cents has become more than $50 million. See the workings in the table below. The students are usually gobsmacked by their findings.

DAY	AMOUNT ADDED	TOTAL AMOUNT
Day 1	$ 0.05	$0.05
Day 2	$ 0.10	$ 0.15
Day 3	$ 0.20	$ 0.35
Day 4	$ 0.40	$ 0.75
Day 5	$ 0.80	$ 1.55
Day 6	$ 1.60	$ 3.15
Day 7	$ 3.20	$ 6.35
Day 8	$ 6.40	$ 12.75
Day 9	$ 12.80	$ 25.55
Day 10	$ 25.60	$ 51.15
Day 11	$ 51.20	$ 102.35
Day 12	$ 102.40	$ 204.75
Day 13	$ 204.80	$ 409.55
Day 14	$ 409.60	$ 819.15
Day 15	$ 819.20	$ 1,638.35
Day 16	$ 1,638.40	$ 3,276.75
Day 17	$ 3,276.80	$ 6,553.55
Day 18	$ 6,553.60	$ 13,107.15
Day 19	$ 13,107.20	$ 26,214.35
Day 20	$ 26,214.40	$ 52,428.75
Day 21	$ 52,428.80	$ 104,857.55
Day 22	$ 104,857.60	$ 209,715.15
Day 23	$ 209,715.20	$ 419,430.35
Day 24	$ 419,430.40	$ 838,860.75
Day 25	$ 838,860.80	$ 1,677,721.55
Day 26	$ 1,677,721.60	$ 3,355,443.15

Day 27	$	3,355,443.20	$	6,710,886.35
Day 28	$	6,710,886.40	$	13,421,772.75
Day 29	$	13,421,772.80	$	26,843,545.55
Day 30	$	26,843,545.60	$	53,687,091.15

But isn't this pretty much how real-life works? Those who delay gratification add value. At first no one notices that healthy meal, the extra hour of study or the little bit of extra training. In some cases, it may take years. This requires grit- intensity and direction of effort (doing the bit extra) as well as the duration of effort (consistency of helpful choices over a period of time). However, those people who are prepared to be gritty and consistently do a little bit extra will eventually attain the slight edge so the compound effect works in their favour.

Aggregation of marginal gains

In 2010, Dave Brailsford took over as General Manager and Performance Director for Team Sky (Great Britain's professional cycling team). At that time, no British cyclist had ever won the Tour de France. Brailsford had a plan to change that. He suggested that by improving everything the team did by just one percent, they would make a remarkable improvement. He believed that if his plan worked, they would achieve the goal of winning the Tour de France in five years' time.

So they optimised everything they could – at first focusing on diet, then the training program then the bike seat and then the tyres. They improved each of these elements by just one percent. "But Brailsford and his team didn't stop there. They searched for 1 percent improvements in tiny areas that were overlooked by almost everyone else: discovering the pillow that offered the best sleep and taking it with them to hotels, testing for the most effective type of massage gel, and teaching riders the best way to wash their hands to avoid infection. They searched for 1 percent improvements everywhere." (Clear, 2014)

They worked towards winning the Tour de France in five years. However, by making very small incremental improvements that others overlooked, they achieved their goal in only three years. In the same year (2012), the British cycling team won 70 percent of the Olympic cycling gold medals. They followed this up by winning the Tour de France the next year as well.

The impact of a one percent improvement has a compound effect over time. Most people who have achieved great things haven't just decided to do something and then pull it off. They have identified small improvements that others have overlooked and made them over a long period of time. Their progress (beyond the norm) may have been very slow at first, but after a period of time they become high achievers in their field.

How can our children be gritty if they don't understand how the slight edge, the compound effect and the accumulation of marginal gains work? Every student should be familiar with these small principles before they leave high school. Otherwise, they won't learn them or they will learn them later in life and lose the benefits of the compounding effect. Results, and the accomplishment of our goals, flow from the life we live on a daily basis. This leads us to the subject of mastery through deliberate practice.

MASTERY THROUGH DELIBERATE PRACTICE

"It is human nature to want to practise what you can already do well, since it's a hell of a lot less work, and a hell of a lot more fun."—Sam Snead, golf champion.

In order for our students to achieve their capabilities, we must encourage them to be gritty. Another method for fostering grit is to unpack the myth of talent by offering a more reliable and evidence-based alternative. For most students, becoming an "expert" is not necessarily the goal. Many would argue that our school system should not attempt to create world champion sports people, musicians or mathematicians. I would agree with that. Rather than being world-champions, students are better off committing to learning and continuous improvement in order to discover and achieve their personal best – whatever that might be. However, we can all learn from the best by creating opportunities to thrive. We must equip all our children so they can unleash their personal potential. If we are going to teach them something, we might as well not teach them about the myth of talent. To this end, we will focus on mastery through deliberate practice.

What is deliberate practice?

Deliberate practice focuses on tasks beyond our current level of competence and comfort. It requires "considerable, specific and sustained effort to do something you can't do well – or even at all" (Ericsson, Prietula & Cokely, 2007). It is highly concentrated, mindful practice. There is a saying, "practice makes perfect", but I strongly disagree with this. When most people practice, they focus on things they already know how to do. If our practice is lazy and unfocused, we will learn poor habits and our performance could actually decrease as a result. There is another saying: "perfect practice makes perfect". Once again I disagree. We can't be perfect when we are really stretching ourselves to new levels. We will make mistakes – many of them. We will need to receive feedback and correct our mistakes – constantly refining our performance. We will need the support of teachers, mentors and coaches to teach us, as we often "don't know what we don't know".

Deliberate practice requires a great deal of grit because it demands full attention and focus. You might recall that the gritty kids who were the highest performers on the national spelling bee had also been prepared to tackle the hardest and least pleasurable problems (Duckworth, 2007). They were prepared to stretch themselves out of their comfort zones. In effect, they were prepared to undergo deliberate practice. That is the only way we can truly get better. Based on studies of expert athletes, novelists and musicians, it appears that after a certain amount of time spent deliberately practising, the quality of our focus can diminish to a point where the practice is no longer useful (Ericsson, Prietula & Cokely, 2007). After this point, the practice is no longer "deliberate", instead it is simply an exercise in discipline (which has value, but not to the same extent as deliberate practice). This has implications for the kids that push themselves too hard, and also for those that believe that an "all-nighter" before an exam is going to help their performance. Rather than "practice makes perfect" or "perfect practice makes perfect", I believe the saying "deliberate practice makes improvement" has much more merit.

Mastery and elite performers

Mastery, or expert performance, is the result of deliberate practice and coaching, not innate skill or talent. Multiple studies have investigated the performance of people who have achieved "elite" levels of performance (Bloom, 1985; Ericsson, Prietula & Cokely, 2007). Consistently and overwhelmingly, the evidence showed that expertise is always grown or developed, not given at birth. In 1985, Bloom's study focused on elite performers across six fields: concert pianists, sculptors, Olympic swimmers, top tennis players, research mathematicians and research neurologists. In each field, 24 people were invited to participate in the study, and a total of 120 people agreed (all of whom met the elite performance criteria). Surprisingly, Bloom's work found no early indicators that could have predicted expert performance. Only ten percent of these individuals had progressed far enough by age 12 for anyone to make confident predictions about their future, world-class performance.

Expert performers did however, share common roots, regardless of their field. There were three commonalities between all elite performers in the study:
- They had practised extensively;
- They had studied with devoted teachers; and
- They had been supported enthusiastically by families during their developing years.

Later research revealed that it was the amount and quality of the practice that were critical factors in the level of expertise people achieved. The studies concluded that "experts are always made, not born".

A walk through the research

Research on expert performance and expertise (Chi, Glaser & Farr, 1988; Ericsson & Smith, 1991) has shown that important characteristics of experts' superior performance are acquired through experience and that the effect of practice on performance is "larger than earlier believed possible" (Ericsson, Krampe, & Tesch-Romer, 1993).

In 1993, Anders Ericsson led a study at the elite, Berlin Academy of Music (Ericsson, Krampe, & Tesch-Romer, 1993). The first part of the study was to split the school's violinists into three groups. The first group comprised of those judged by their professors to be future world class soloists. As there were only 10 who qualified for this group, they limited the size of the other two groups to ten participants as well to ensure validity of the experiment. The second group was comprised of those who were predicted to be excellent professional musicians, while the third group was comprised of those predicted to be great amateur musicians. The musicians were all asked the same question: over the course of your career, (since you first picked up the violin) how many hours have you practised? They found that each member of group one (world class soloists) had already completed 10,000 hours or more of purposeful, single-minded practice. The second group (excellent professional musicians) had completed roughly 8,000 hours, while the third group (great amateur musicians) had completed just over 4,000 hours. Accomplished individuals work day after day, for at least 10 or 15 years, to reach the top of their fields. In other words, even the most gifted performers need a minimum of 10,000 hours of intense practice before they win international competitions (Ericsson, Prietula, & Cokely, 2007).

Another myth busted by this study was the idea of "naturals" and "grinds". It is interesting to note that the researchers could not find a single "natural" in the academy. A natural in this sense is a violinist who floats seamlessly to the top and who practises a fraction of the time their peers do. Nor could they find any "grinds" people who worked harder than everyone else but didn't have what it takes to reach the top. The research suggests that once a musician has enough talent to make it to a top music school, the factor that distinguishes one performer from another is how hard he or she has worked (Gladwell, 2008).

Why does it work?

Deliberate practice works because it gives the brain the time it needs to adapt to elite levels of performance. Matthew Syed, in his book *Bounce,* argues that most world class performers act on autopilot. Top tennis players subconsciously read the play based on the body movements of the other players. Essentially, they have a good idea how the ball will be hit by their opponent before they make contact with the ball. These subtleties are learned over time. World class tennis is not related to extreme levels of reflex; it is the reading of the play that makes some players seem to have all the time in the world (this can be noticed in just about every sport). Deliberate practice works because it gives the brain the time it needs to respond to demands placed upon it. This occurs through the process of neuroplasticity (as explained earlier in part two). The synapses that need to refine their processes so they fire together must be trained to do so. The myelination that allows for the transfer of information from one neuron to another also takes time to develop. Through the process of deliberate practice, we direct the focus of neuroplasticity to the areas that most need to adapt. Neurologist Daniel Levitin states that "in study after study, this number (10,000 hours or about 10 years) comes up again and again. It seems that it takes the brain this long to assimilate all that it needs to know to achieve true mastery" (Levitin, 2007). This is true for everyone including Mozart, Tiger Woods and Einstein.

Golf champion Sam Snead was said to have one of the most beautiful swings in the sport. He was regularly called "the best natural player ever". But Snead said of himself, "practice puts brains in your muscles. People always said I had a natural swing. When I was young, I'd play and practise all day, and into the night. My hands bled. Nobody worked harder at golf than I did." Rewiring the brain through deliberate practice seems to be a vehicle for moving to the top, but there are other factors at play.

Relative age effect

Malcolm Gladwell's book, *Outliers–the story of success,* suggests that one's date of birth has an impact on the level of success one experiences in particular sports. In many sports there is an overrepresentation of players born shortly after the cut-off date (at the start of the year or season) and an underrepresentation of players born shortly before the cut-off date. He cites the example of elite Canadian hockey players. Roughly 40 percent are born between January and March, 30 percent between April and June, 20 percent between July and September and 10 percent between October and December.

One of the major studies the relative age effect area focuses on two sports: soccer and ice hockey. For example, in soccer, the phenomenon occurs in the first and second professional soccer divisions in Belgium, the Netherlands and France. It is also evidenced in the four highest professional soccer leagues in England. Other sports that feature this statistical anomaly are cricket, baseball and tennis (Musch & Grondin, 2001).

When I came across this research, I decided to compare it with Australian data. So I went online in search of the 2015 NRL players' birth dates (NRL Player Birthdays, n.d.). It was interesting to note that at the time, the data from Australian NRL players seemed to replicate the findings from other countries and sports (but to a lesser degree). In particular, most players were born in the quarter between January and March (190) and the least number of players were born between October and December (137). 140 players were born between April and June, while 138 players were born between July and September. This means that January, February and March have a 35 percent better representation than any other quarter. In any two-month period, January and February had the most number of players (138), while November and December had the least (82). More players were born in January

(72) than any other month, closely followed by February (66), while November had the least number of players in the NRL (33). This seems to indicate that being born in the first few months of the year gives players a higher chance of making it to the NRL and supports the findings from other research.

Why does this happen?

Children play sport with other children born in the same 12-month period as them (based on the cut-off dates for that sport). Prior to, and during, adolescence, a difference of six to ten months in age represents an enormous amount of physical maturity. When the first representative teams are being picked in any given sport, physical maturity plays a big part. Coaches will usually choose the stronger, faster, more coordinated competitors, but what they don't consider is the relative age effect – the fact that some players could be nearly 12 months younger than their bigger, stronger peers. You will agree that the differences between a 20 year old and a 30 year old are not as marked. However, anyone who works with adolescents (or anyone who has adolescent kids or has been an adolescent!) can tell you that significant development and maturing can occur in a very small amount of time. Coaches unknowingly choose the older players (those born close to the start of the cut-off period).

These slightly older, bigger, stronger kids are given the best coaching, the best opportunities and access to facilities. They receive the same club training as other kids, as well as the additional time training and playing for the "rep" team. The level of competition they are exposed to is higher than their younger club team mates and they are continually challenged to raise their game. The effect compounds. Back in their club team they are stand outs, which leads to more time on the field as opposed to the bench with their slightly younger, smaller, weaker teammates. This also gives them the opportunity to appreciate the game more and be more motivated to continue to keep at it. Research also shows that the younger children (those born close to the end of the cut-off) are more likely to drop out of the sport (Musch & Grondin, 2001).

"The training time difference among children may also be magnified by the fact that relatively older players are more likely to be chosen for select teams and high ability groups. Such selection is not only associated with receiving better coaching and facing better opponents; being involved in higher competition levels is in itself more prestigious and therefore likely to increase motivation. Thus, if, in a coach's mind, two children are considered to have the same age because they are born in the same year, the child born in January has a huge advantage over the other, first, in chances to be part of the team if too many children compete for limited places on a team, and second, in active participation in the games" (Musch & Grondin, 2001). This leads to the anomaly we see in the dates of birth of elite sportspeople from a range of sports. The effect is particularly pronounced where the sport draws from a very large talent pool, and where the access to facilities (for example, ice skating rinks or coaches) is somewhat limited.

Ultimately, the relative age effect is another example of the value of deliberate practice. The connection between the two is that without getting into the early representative teams during the developmental years, the younger players (for their age group) won't get the extra practice. Without the extra practice a sportsperson is unlikely to get 10,000 hours of deliberate practice before the professional teams begin to select the very best youth players to join their ranks.

Teaching students about deliberate practice will add to their grit account. They can use deliberate practice to work towards the achievement of the goals that are most important to them.

GOAL SETTING

Goal setting actually works. In our world, we are overstimulated and distracted. We can choose to do everything at a satisfactory level, or we can choose to do just a few things at a very high level. We should first limit the scope of our efforts then watch those efforts have a desired effect (Achor, 2010). This requires priorities and focus – this requires goals. Goals give us the focus we need to direct our time, energy and effort towards things that are most valuable to us. However, in order to set and achieve worthwhile goals, we must understand and apply three concepts. These are the reticular activating system (RAS), mental contrasting and implementation intentions (MCII) and process-focus. I will explain each in turn.

The reticular activating system (RAS)

The RAS is a place where we receive information about the internal and external experiences of our world. Essentially, it is a filter for our five senses. The mind receives more than one million pieces of information every second. This is a lot to process and is impossible even for the remarkable human conscious mind. However, the RAS filters the information. It ensures that the bulk of the information perceived by our senses is relegated to our subconscious mind. It allows us to consciously process a tiny fraction of the information we receive. Only about 120 pieces of information per second are sent to the conscious mind (a tiny fraction of that perceived by our senses). Simply put, the RAS only lets through information important to us – particularly information that is either of value or is a threat. Without the RAS, our minds would be bombarded with too much information and the result would be a lack of clarity. The RAS has been compared to a camera lens that focuses on a particular subject and blurs the rest of the unnecessary things into the background of the picture (James, n.d.).

Here is an example. A few years ago my wife and I were looking to buy her a new car. We were after a small family car – not too small to make it impractical, but not too big to make it too bulky to handle. We had decided that a Toyota Corolla would be ideal. We went to a government auction to see if we could pick one up for the right price. It was amazing; everyone seemed to want a Toyota Corolla. All the bidders kept bumping up the price so we left the auction disappointed and empty handed. I was explaining this to a mate the next weekend and he asked if we really wanted a Toyota, or just that style of car. I explained that we really just wanted the right sized car to meet our needs as we had started a family. He mentioned that a Nissan Tiida might be suitable. Neither my wife nor I had heard of a Nissan Tiida before. I was astonished at what happened during the course of the next two weeks. Without even looking for them, I came across three Nissan Tiidas. Once at the petrol station – filling up at the next bowser, once on my way to work – pulling up behind one at a set of lights, and once at the shopping centre – walking past it on the way into the shops. Nothing had changed. I didn't change the petrol station, the shop I visited or my route to work. To my knowledge, there hadn't just been a new release of Nissan Tiidas in Australia. It was business as usual. They had always been there, but I had never noticed them. Prior to that conversation with my friend, Nissan Tiidas were not important to me, so my RAS had relegated this car to my subconscious mind. It filtered them out. But as soon as they were of value to me, I noticed them everywhere. For the record: a few weeks later we bought a Nissan Tiida.

As I facilitate sessions with school staff and students, I often tell this story and then ask whether anyone has experienced a similar thing. In every group, most students and staff will raise their hand and offer their own examples. Many of the staff explain they had thought this meant something was "meant to be" or "a stroke of coincidence".

The implication is that whatever we focus on is what we'll tend to see. If we are looking for problems, or road blocks, we will find them. If we are looking for faults in others, we will find them. If we are looking for opportunities, possibilities, things to be grateful for, we will find them (I discuss this in the gratitude section later). If we are looking for ways to achieve our goals, we will find them. And this is why goal setting is powerful.

Mental contrasting and implementation intentions (MCII)

Adolescents can struggle with setting or striving for goals that require a great deal of persistence. While schools often invite students to "dream big dreams", "shoot for the moon" and "think positive", rarely does this seem to be reflected in student outcomes. Goal setting will not work in this context. However, projecting towards a desired future state, expecting setbacks along the way, and creating a plan for continuing towards a goal is much more effective. Mental contrasting and implementation intentions have been found to enhance this process. Mental contrasting is the process of contrasting our desired future state (the goal), with the obstacles that may stand in the way. Mental contrasting enhances the goal setting stage and strengthens goal commitment. While setting goals and committing to them does not turn them into a reality, the process of mental contrasting has been found to energise individuals into taking action (Oettingen, et al., 2009).

Once goals are set, we must then strive for them. While goal setting is enhanced through mental contrasting, goal striving is enhanced by forming implementation intentions. Essentially, this process requires making "if/then" plans and has been shown to enhance our ability to get started or stay on track with the actions required to bring goals to fruition (Gollwitzer, 1999). This plan can detail when, where and how the individual will take action. In a study of students preparing for a high stakes exam, used to determine merit-based scholarships, those students who were taught mental contrasting and implementation intentions completed over 60 percent more practice questions than students in the control condition (Duckworth, Grant, Loew, Oettingen, & Gollwitzer, 2011), Rather than "shoot for the moon", mental contrasting and implementation intentions has proven results.

There are some very good support materials available for this. One such tool is an app called WOOP (wish, outcome, obstacle, plan), which is based on 20 years of scientific research by creator Gabriele Oettingen. This app supports people through the process of mental contrasting in the first three steps. The fourth, and final, step is essentially creating an implementation intention. Here's how it works: You first name a wish, then you name the best possible outcome, then you name your main obstacle, and as a last step you make an (if/then) plan. The following elaborates on this process, and can be taught to students of all ages to enhance their academic results (in fact anyone can apply this to all areas of life).

The WOOP process:
1. WISH – What is your most important wish or concern in your professional life? (pick something challenging but that you can fulfil in the next month)
2. OUTCOME – What would be the best thing about fulfilling your wish? How would it make you feel?
3. OBSTACLE – What is the main obstacle that stands in the way of you fulfilling your wish?
4. PLAN- What can you do to overcome that obstacle? (Name an action you can take). Your plan will take this form... If (obstacle), then I will (take this action).

Focus on process, not product

In order for students to achieve their goals, they must be process-focused, not product focused. In particular, they must begin to value a journey of slow growth, rather than getting to a destination quickly. The desire to achieve results quickly fools us into thinking that the result is the prize, when in reality it is the working towards something of value that enhances our lives. Too often, after people have achieved a goal (for example to lose eight kilograms), they will revert to old ways of thinking and doing. This reverting back leads them to undo their good work, and the result they had worked so hard for. This creates a "yo-yo" effect. A better goal may be to consider the sort of person we want to be. That is, we might want to be a healthy person, or someone who exercises four or five times a week. This is not a destination goal; rather it is a process goal. It is a matter of continually doing the actions that lead to the desired results. Focusing on a process is a great way to keep a scorecard of our goals, as well as to continue the journey beyond the realisation of a goal.

Another way to think about this is to focus on the practice, rather than on the performance. For example, if a sports team wants to win a grand final, they should focus on what they do at practice each day. If an adult wants to lose weight, he or she should focus on their daily nutrition and exercise program. If students want to achieve academic success, they should focus on improving the quality and regularity of their study. In each of these examples, focusing on the process allows for improvement and makes the achievement of the goal possible. After the goal has been attained, in most cases real learners and improvers want to build on that accomplishment. If we don't hold on too tightly to the need for immediate results, we can continue on a growth journey for the long-term.

Goals are great for prompting us to take action towards a desired future state. Your goal is like a compass that gives you direction, rather than a destination with buried treasure. Goals can also be likened to the rudder on a boat, while the actions we take (or the process) are like the engine. While the rudder (the goal) is essential for setting the direction, it is the engine (the process of making relevant daily actions) that moves the boat forward.

A key strategy for building these desired daily actions is forming effective habits.

HABIT FORMATION

"We are what we repeatedly do. Excellence, then, is not an act, but a habit."—Aristotle

Habits are responses that are activated automatically. These responses are usually activated by cues that have occurred simultaneously with responses in the past. In Charles Duhigg's best seller *The power of habit*, he defines habits as "the choices all of us deliberately make at some point, and then stop thinking about but continue doing, often everyday" (Duhigg, 2013). William James once said that we are "mere bundles of habit" (James, 1984). We know from the section on the compound effect that our daily actions can have a great impact on our lives when the effect is compounded over time. A Duke University study has shown that it is "actually people's unthinking routines—or habits—that form the bedrock of everyday life. Without habits, people would be doomed to plan, consciously guide, and monitor every action" (Neal, Wood, & Quinn, 2006). Neural evidence indicates that with repetition the brain "chunks" whole sequences of responses. Essentially, our habits form over time as repeated thoughts or actions lead to strengthened neural connections. This means that "habits require limited conscious control to proceed to completion" (Neal, Wood, & Quinn, 2006). The behaviour becomes automatic. By understanding this pattern and how it works, we can rebuild these patterns in any way we choose.

"People often fail in their attempts at changing everyday lifestyle habits such as their diet and level of exercise. Such failures are understandable given that cues such as time of day and location trigger repetition of past responses. Failures to change do not necessarily indicate poor willpower, but instead the power of situations to trigger past responses. Habits keep us doing what we have always done" (Neal, Wood, & Quinn, 2006). Many of the decisions we make each day are habitual. One study suggests that approximately 45 percent of our everyday actions are habits in the sense that they are performed almost daily and usually in the same location (Wood, Quinn, & Kashy, 2002). Habits make our life easier as we don't need to invest a lot of energy and effort into doing them. Habitual behaviour has been linked to reduced stress when compared to non-habitual behaviour. It is believed the reason for this is that less thought is necessary to guide our actions when behaving habitually (Wood, Quinn, & Kashy, 2002). When a habit emerges, our brain stops fully participating in decision making (Duhigg, 2013). However, our brain can't tell the difference between good habits and bad ones – which means that our habits can work for us, or against us. For this reason if we want to create positive results in our lives, "we should make our nervous system our ally, instead of our enemy" (James, 1984). In order to be gritty and achieve more success, we can form habits that work in our favour. In order to do this, we must understand the habit loop, keystone habits and choice architecture.

Habit loop

Our habits can be broken into three steps:
1. The trigger: the event that starts the habit (triggers could include time of day, other people, a location, a preceding event or an emotional state).
2. The routine: the behaviour that you perform (the habit itself).
3. The reward: the benefit that is associated with the behaviour.

When we want to begin a new habit or cease an existing one, we use the habit loop. For example, if I would like to meditate more regularly (this is step 2, the routine), I must find an appropriate trigger. For example, when I put the keys in the ignition of my car each morning (this is step 1, the trigger), I will meditate for one minute. If I would like to practice gratitude (the routine) more regularly, I should align it to an appropriate trigger. This might be brushing my teeth, getting into bed or putting on my shoes. New habits that we create should be small and easy to follow, so that we can achieve small wins and begin to strengthen the habit loop. Yet another example would be linking a new desired routine (going to the gym) to a regular daily trigger (driving home from work). If we are trying to cease an existing habit, like eating less chocolate, we should identify our triggers and replace the routine. For example, if I usually get peckish about an hour after lunch each day (the trigger) and begin looking for a snack, I should instead ensure that I have a healthy snack on hand. I will still get the same trigger, but I have replaced the existing routine with something more desirable. It is far more effective to replace existing negative habits than it is to eliminate them.

Keystone habits

Some habits are strongly linked to other habits. These are called "keystone habits". For example, if I am able to stick to the (keystone) habit of getting up and doing some exercise, it has a flow-on effect throughout my day. Typically, after exercise my body craves good food rather than junk. It has me feeling energised, focused and more productive at work. Due to the exercise, I sleep better at night. One habit is linked to a number of others.

Someone might replace smoking with walking. This would have a have a flow-on effect. The change of the keystone habit may lead to a change in diet, working, sleeping, saving money, scheduling worktime, planning for the future and so on.

This works at the organisational level too. For example, Alcoa used this in the 1990s to focus on becoming one of the safest companies in the USA. Not only did this focus on safety lead to huge improvements in the safety of employees, but the flow-on effect was huge: increases in income and profits, share prices increased 500 percent in 13 years and increased market capitalisation. It was one of the best performing companies in the American stock market during that time. Essentially the attack on one habit led to a standard of excellence in the company, as the changes rippled throughout the company. The focus on improved safety led to natural improvements in the efficiency, effectiveness and quality of the overall production process. Paul O'Neill, the CEO of Alcoa during the period from 1987-2000 believed that "if I could start disrupting habits around one thing, it would spread throughout the entire company". He believed that some habits have the power to start a chain reaction, and he was right. These are keystone habits. These habits start a process that transforms everything in a company or in a life. Keystone habits allow us to focus our energy and attention on just a couple of areas, and the flow-on effect takes it to many other areas.

For students, one keystone habit that I have noticed over the years is the regular use of the student diary. If they have a system in place for managing and recording their responsibilities and learning tasks, they tend to cope with the demands much better. This keystone habit can have a flow-on effect into all other areas of their life.

As parents and educators, we should consider keystone habits in our own lives. This will help us to live more fulfilling lives and to model good habits to the children we care about. We also have the opportunity to help our children or students to identify some keystone habits in their own lives that will lead them towards fulfilment and satisfaction.

Choice architecture

"Chains of habit are too light to be felt until they are too heavy to be broken."—Warren Buffet

We cannot rely on willpower in order to stick to good habits. Research has shown that over time, our willpower can become used up, or depleted, much like tired muscles (Baumeister & Tierney, 2012). In a study using chocolate chip cookies and unsolvable problems, participants were divided into three groups. It was found that people who were told not to eat the chocolate chip cookies in front of them gave up very easily on the subsequent unsolvable puzzles. Those who were allowed to eat the chocolate chip cookies, or who had no chocolate chip cookies in sight, lasted much longer than those who could see them and were required to use willpower to deny themselves. Not only does this study show that willpower can be depleted, it also shows that choice architecture can help preserve our willpower.

It has also been found that only 20 percent of dieters are able to keep off the lost weight for any extended length of time (Ansel, 2009). Relying on willpower and a dose of motivation, goal setting or even a New Year's resolution doesn't seem to work in most cases. We need more than this – and so do the students that we teach. We need to carefully design our default choices – making it easier to make the right decisions impulsively. "When your willpower is depleted, you are even more likely to make decisions based on the environment around you. After all, if you're feeling drained, stressed, or overwhelmed then you're not going to go through a lot of effort to cook a healthy dinner or fit in a workout. You'll grab whatever is easiest" (Clear, 2014). Choice architecture is about designing our environment so that the default choice we make (the easiest choice) is a better one. For example, placing healthy foods in more visible spots in the fridge, pantry or even on the bench and moving less healthy food options out of sight.

An example of an individual who may have depleted their willpower would be a worker in times of stress. In this situation, an employee will use all of their willpower to work hard, and everything else collapses as a result. They are able to muster up the energy to get out of bed early and get to work but their diet goes downhill. They will do what they need to do, however, not have any extra willpower to do the things that align with their core values such as spending quality time with family, eating well or exercising. At these times, it can all seem too much. Their will power reserves are depleted.

For teachers, end of semester one reporting deadlines are a difficult time. We must appear as though we have it all under control. However, the reality is that we need to assess, mark and report on all of our kids – while simultaneously planning, teaching and carrying out business as usual. However, every member of the school is experiencing the same raised levels of stress (staff and students alike). Schools can be a terrifying place at this time! In any case, during this period of assessing, reporting and continued teaching, many teachers experience depleted willpower. It requires so much of them to carry out their work responsibilities that their regular diet and exercise regimes can very easily be abandoned. In these cases, we need choice architecture.

A study at Massachusetts General Hospital, aimed at helping people make better food choices by using choice architecture (Thorndike, Sonnenberg, Riis, Barraclough, & Levy, 2012). Simply by adding fridges filled with water, and putting water in baskets around the hospital cafeteria, customers changed their buying habits for better. In only three months, soft drink sales dropped by 11.4 percent. Meanwhile, bottled water sales increased by 25.8 percent. People made better choices as the default choice was improved.

In order to preserve your willpower for when you need it most, you can use choice architecture. Doing so will ensure that the environment you surround yourself with will ultimately lead to positive default actions. On a cold winter morning, I would prefer to stay in bed than to get out, get dressed and go for a run. However, I have found that if I put my shoes, socks and running clothes beside my bed it is much easier to throw them on and get out there. Doing so improves my default choice – this is choice architecture. I have already started the process of doing a workout the night before (by getting the clothes ready) and I simply need to finish what I started.

Mihaly Csikszentmihayli has coined the term "activation energy" to describe what is similar to the term inertia (Csikszentmihayli, 1997). However, instead of referring to the tendency of an object to remain at rest or moving on its current path, activation energy refers to our actions and choices which take the path of least resistance. Inactivity is the easiest option. Therefore, how can we use this concept to assist us in the default choices we make? It is simple- we can use what Shawn Achor refers to as the "20-second rule". He suggests lowering the activation energy for habits you want to adopt and raising it for habits you want to avoid. "The more we can lower or even eliminate the activation energy for our desired actions, the more we enhance our ability to jump-start positive change" (Achor, 2010). If you want to watch TV less often and read more instead, put the remote control inside a drawer rather than on the coffee table – and then put a book on the coffee table. Whenever you sit on the couch ready to watch TV, your default choice now becomes reading a book. It only takes 20 seconds to get the remote out of the drawer, however, it has increased the activation energy required. I also use this strategy by putting beer in the downstairs fridge, not in the kitchen. There are times when the activation energy required to go and get a beer to have with dinner actually means that I change my choice to water instead (as it is readily available in the kitchen). Once again, it only takes 20 seconds, but it is enough.

During work, I am tempted to check my emails regularly, which I know is not the best use of my time. This has led me to closing down Microsoft Outlook after I have done my regular scheduled emailing. The extra 20 seconds it takes for Microsoft Outlook to load is a wonderful deterrent to me and helps me stay on track with my work. Having some fresh fruit on the bench in a fruit bowl, rather than in the crisper in the fridge reduces the activation energy required to make a good choice of snack. Combine that with making unhealthy snacks harder to access (or getting rid of them altogether) and it becomes much easier to make great choices. You can use this knowledge in order to support your best decision making. For students, it may involve making the bed each morning, or ensuring that their school locker is tidy, organised and structured. They can then carry this composure and organisation with them to their classes. Parents and educators can also use choice architecture in study environments, study schedules or daily routines with children and students. Our attention now turns from managing our environment, to managing our energy and effort.

EFFORT AND ENERGY MANAGEMENT

In order for anyone to thrive, they must manage their energy and effort. Many of us try to manage our time but are ineffective. There are only so many hours in a day and once you have worked as hard, fast and long as you possibly can, there is not much more you can squeeze out of a day, before screwing over yourself or your family. I know – I worked that way for a long time. Never once did time stop for me so I could leave work on time thinking "there is nothing more for me to do at the office". And to top it all off, I have gradually learned over my working life (I am a slow learner!) that there is no prize for being busy. So we can stop trying to manage time. We must accomplish more with less. We must seek to be effective rather than efficient. Efficiency requires us to find faster ways to do the same things, while effectiveness is about working smarter by using priorities and being selective about what we do. Being effective is about managing our energy and effort. One of the secrets to effective effort and energy management is letting go of what is less important to focus on the more important. The Pareto principle is a helpful concept in this regard, as is the bower bird model (referred to later in Part 5 on implementation).

The Pareto principle has also been called the "80/20 Principle" or the "law of the vital few". It was first noted in research by Vilfredo Pareto in 1896 when he realised that approximately 80 percent of the land in Italy was owned by 20 percent of the population. Since then, many other scholars have found that a similar trend applies to economics, business, sales, occupational health and safety and computing.

Some examples are:

- The richest 20 percent of the world's population control 82.7 percent of the world's income (Program, 1992)
- Software companies have noted that by fixing the top 20 percent of the most-reported bugs, 80percent of the related errors and crashes in a given system would be eliminated (Rooney, 2002)
- Roughly 80 percent of a company's profits come from 20 percent of its customers
- Roughly 80 percent of a company's sales come from 20 percent of its products
- Roughly 80 percent of a company's sales are made by 20 percent of its sales staff (Koch, 2011)
- Roughly 20 percent of the hazards in a workplace will account for 80 percent of the injuries (Woodcock, 2010)

This can be applied to our own lives as educators and parents. I have noticed that this is an area requiring attention in schools. It is a matter of setting our priorities and acknowledging that some things are of less value than others. As educators, we have a heart for helping children. However, many of us are burnt out by the effort and energy required. The school yard is not usually a nice place in week 8 or 9 of a school term. The staff room is a little bit the same. I mean no offence to educators – we do our best in trying times. It is easy to get overwhelmed by the constant barrage of jobs that come our way. We must realise that we can't help if we don't look after ourselves. We must remind ourselves that not all help is equal. We need to set priorities before we try to work harder, faster and longer to get the work done.

A useful tool for managing our energy and efforts is the Eisenhower Matrix (popularised by Stephen Covey in *The 7 Habits of Highly Effective People*). See the image facing.

Eisenhower Matrix	URGENT	LESS URGENT
IMPORTANT	Quadrant 1- Do first	Quadrant 2- Schedule
LESS IMPORTANT	Quadrant 3- Delegate	Quadrant 4- Eliminate

(Source: Andreas Kwiatkowski- https://www.youtube.com watch?v=tT89OZ7TNwc)

The distinction is made between activities that are important and those which are urgent. Dwight Eisenhower once said, "What's important is seldom urgent, and what's urgent is seldom important."

A quick summary of each quadrant is:

Quadrant 1 – Important and urgent – do first: review important document for principal, ensure reports are completed on time, call back a parent who had a concern about a bullying incident.

Quadrant 2 – Important and less urgent – schedule: go to the gym, professional reading, family holidays.

Quadrant 3 – Less important but urgent – delegate: any emails, any task that can be reasonably passed on to someone else in your organisation (this depends on the role you hold). For example, an assistant/deputy principal delegating the bulk of the work of a high school supervision roster to an administrative team member.

Quadrant 4 – Less important and less urgent – eliminate: surfing the internet, social media, TV, procrastination.

Important activities are aligned to our personal or professional goals and should receive our attention. Even though they don't necessarily act on us (that is, they don't have to be done right now or today), they do need to be treated as priorities. Those urgent activities in our schedules are not closely aligned to our goals and should either be delegated (if possible) or eliminated. We must place our top priorities into our schedules first and work on them in order to get the highest return on investment. We should work on our tasks in the order of the quadrants. However for many people, there is a tendency to work on urgent tasks (quadrants 1 and 3) first and then complete the less urgent tasks (quadrants 2 and 4) later. The trouble is some of our very top priorities fall into quadrant 2. For example planning, preparation, health and wellbeing, investing into important parts of our job, developing skills, learning, professional development and spending time with family. We never need to do them now, which leads to us putting them off until all urgent tasks are completed. The trouble is, there is usually not enough time in the day to complete all tasks, and therefore the important, less urgent quadrant 2 tasks can get left undone. In this case, we will be busy but less effective. You can see how priorities are so important.

Warren Buffet's model supports this, but is even simpler. He has been quoted as asking an employee to write down their 25 most important goals. Then he asked them to circle the most important five. Then he directs them to put their energy and effort into the first five. The next 20 (numbers six to 25) are on a list of their own, called the "avoid at all costs" list. It might feel nice to get some of these things done, but it comes at a cost. The cost is less time to spend on the top priorities. We must remember that each time we say yes to something, we say no to something else.

As educators and parents, we need to invite young people to set priorities based on their goals. Then they need to be very discerning. Effort and energy management is particularly important for those who are involved in everything. They are sporty, musical, friendly, academic and generally hard working kids who are likely to be the current or future school leaders. If we don't equip these students with the skills they need in energy and effort management, their schedules will crush them and they will achieve far less than their potential.

Applying what has been learned in the classroom

When it comes to teaching this to students, I ask them to first determine priority areas, develop goals (as discussed earlier), then key actions. At this point, they are ready to attempt prioritising a weekly schedule by using the "big rocks" method, which involves them putting in their top priorities first. They must also nominate at least one activity which they consider destroys their time. They will replace this activity with something productive – rewiring the brain by attending to the habit loop. If their top priorities do not account for the majority of their time, they will not achieve their goals, and realising this could be the first step for many of them. This is where delayed gratification, the compound effect, goal setting and habit formation intersect and become very practical. Then they require the grit to ensure they remain disciplined when other distractions (often called opportunities, parties, Facebook messages) pop up.

A note for educators about effort and energy management

There are so many distractions and interruptions in an average work day. Firstly, there are many emails to manage – with many school personnel receiving more than 100 emails a day. On top of this, there are phone calls (on the work or mobile phone), text messages and visits from co-workers. Add to this the fact that many adults are on social media such which offers further distraction. Technological advances can assist us in our work but they also offer us regular interruptions. While these distractions interrupt us from our work, it is important to acknowledge that sometimes they are our work. For example, a year 9 coordinator attempts to do some work in her office while she has a 20-minute slot at lunchtime. She is not required to supervise students. There is a knock at the door and two year 9 girls are having a "stress attack" about an exam. Alternatively, a primary school principal has scheduled 30 minutes in her office just after lunch only to receive a call from a parent who reports a major bullying issue amongst year 6 girls. These are examples of distractions that are the work of an educator, and are difficult to avoid. However, there are many others that could be avoided.

Research conducted by Gloria Mark from the University of California suggests that once thrown off track, it can take a person 25 minutes to get back on track. In 2004, she studied office workers for over 1,000 hours and also found that the average time between distractions was about 11 minutes (Thompson, 2005). It would be reasonable to assume that with the rise in technology, office workers receive more distractions now than they did in 2004. In our work, we must learn to help ourselves and remove any unnecessary distractions. If we do not, we risk spreading our energy and effort too thin, which will lead to high stress and low output. The research also shows that after "only 20 minutes of interrupted performance people reported significantly higher stress, frustration, workload, effort, and pressure" (Mark, Gudith, & Klocke, 2008).

If you don't have time in your day, work on one thing at a time and remove any unnecessary distraction. Multitasking is a myth. We work better in focused periods where we can do one thing without distraction. Move away from the phone. For teachers, this means turning off the email alerts and scheduling to check it twice a day (for a short amount of time). If you receive an email that requires a lot of work from you (and it is important), schedule it in your calendar and let the person know when you will be completing it. Don't let it take you away from your priorities. We all need to manage our work and not let our work manage us. This leads into our next section on wellbeing.

A final note about grit

Sometimes the grittiest students get hung up on constantly improving their results. In most cases, this is admirable. In some cases (or possibly in all cases at some time), this can lead to stress, anxiety and a lack of mental health. It is important to apply grit with a sense of balance. Young people may find it difficult to know when to "pull back". There is a need to ensure that while we are working hard and sticking with our goals, we are also working on our wellbeing. We must invest in the goose if we want to continue to receive her golden eggs. For parents and teachers, if children display the wonderful qualities of grit, we should continue to promote these in everything we do. However, for their sake, we should also be on the lookout for early warning signs of increased stress, decreasing mental health, and so on that occur as a result of pushing themselves too hard towards certain goals. Skipping meals, excessive fatigue and irritability are just a few of the symptoms that might appear. You know the young people you care about, and you will see the warning signs if you are mindful of them. In the moment, young people may need the guidance and support of a parent, teacher or mentor to help them wade through and prioritise competing needs, before their high levels of grit affect their wellbeing.

If building grit in a school setting is of interest to you, resources and lesson plans are available at: http://www.unleashingpersonalpotential.com.au/

PART FOUR: WELLBEING

- Linking wellbeing to achievement
- Meditation
- Character strengths
- Gratitude
- Interpersonal skills
- Active constructive responding
- Generosity

"Happy, calm students learn best."—Daniel Goleman

LINKING WELLBEING TO ACHIEVEMENT

A 2004 study of Harvard Students found that four out of five suffered from depression at one stage in the academic year, while nearly half of them were so depressed that it impacted their normal functioning (Kaplan, 2004). Depression rates today are nearly ten times higher than they were 50 years ago, while the mean onset age of depression has sunk from 29.5 years to 14.5 years during this period (Seligman, 2002). Whether we like it or not, wellbeing is somewhat counter cultural. Schools and workplaces are not typically overflowing with people who are thriving in terms of their wellbeing – and this has a cost on worker productivity in the corporate world and academic achievement in education. But all of that is really a conversation about disease, not wellbeing.

Martin Seligman is the founder of positive psychology. He was also the academic that gave Geelong Grammar a wonderful reputation on the global stage for their leadership in positive education. Positive Education is focused on developing specific skills that assist students and staff to "strengthen their relationships, build positive emotions, enhance personal resilience, promote mindfulness, and encourage a healthy lifestyle" (Grammar, n.d.). Seligman is a psychologist who became disinterested in studying different pathologies. He chooses to focus on exploring optimal human functioning – flourishing, rather than languishing. Much of the psychological field was particularly focused on trying to get people from poor wellbeing to neutral, or trying to "fix" people. Wellbeing is not just about feeling good; it is not just the absence of pathology and illness. Instead, Seligman focuses on taking people from wherever they are towards wellness. Rather than moving people from -5 to 0, he talks about moving people towards +5. His work has inspired my own passion and commitment for empowering people to live to their full potential. It's about thriving and continuously striving for personal excellence.

Wellbeing is a well-known and well researched determinant of success. It increases our ability to function. According to a meta-analysis involving almost 300 studies and 275,000 people worldwide, wellbeing leads to success in every domain in our lives, including marriage, friendship, careers, businesses, creativity and health (Lyubomirsky, King, & Diener, 2005). Wellbeing leads to thriving in social, work, physical, psychological and personal domains. In one study, the wellbeing of employees was measured, and these employees were followed for 18 months. Those who were happier at the start ended up receiving higher evaluations and more pay later on (Staw, Sutton, & Pelled, 1994). In another study, levels of wellbeing were measured for students starting university. This was found to correlate with their income levels 19 years later (Diener, Nickerson, Lucas, & Sandvik, 2002). Those with high levels of wellbeing also experienced higher job satisfaction and were less likely to have ever been unemployed. Employees with high wellbeing are more productive on the job. Research has shown that those employees who are most unhappy take an extra 15 "sick" days off per year (Index, 2008).

For students who go to school 200 days a year for 13 years, this would equate to an extra 195 days of school missed during their school career. This would put them a year behind their peers by the end of their years at school. I have come across extreme cases where the absentee rate for particular students was more than 50 percent in a semester. This will have a very obvious impact on learning over the duration of a school career. And it would seem that these employees and students are not just taking "sickies" or faking it. Research shows that those with higher wellbeing experience higher resistance to the common cold. In one (slightly unethical) study, researchers measured people's emotional state and then injected them with a strain of the cold virus through nasal drops. A week later, the researchers found that those with higher levels of wellbeing were less affected by the virus. It wasn't just that they felt better. When measured by doctors, their physical symptoms – sneezing, coughing, congestion and inflammation were far less significant (Cohen, Doyle, Turner, Alper, & Skoner, 2003). In a different study of Catholic nuns, researchers found that those who were more overtly joyful in their journals at the age of 20, lived an average of 10 years longer than those who were more neutral or negative in their journals (Danner, Snowdon, & Friesen, 2001).

Based on this research, it is easy to see why wellbeing is an essential ingredient to thriving at school and beyond. Wellbeing for schools is not just about looking after our staff and students by helping them gain more peace, joy and happiness in their lives, although these are important. Wellbeing training for schools equips people with the skills they need to achieve more every day, and so improve performance outcomes for our staff and students. This is why "cutting-edge software companies have foosball tables in their employee lounge, why Yahoo! has an in-house massage parlour and why Google engineers are encouraged to bring their dogs to work" (Achor, 2010). It also explains why top schools such as Geelong Grammar and Brisbane Grammar have embraced positive education. Geelong Grammar have established their own Institute for Positive Education, while Brisbane Grammar values wellbeing so much that they ensure that every Monday morning, their entire school engages in a 50-minute wellbeing lesson – before any other curriculum activities take place.

While some educators believe that a focus on wellbeing takes time and resources away from academic pursuits, these schools are aware of the evidence that "students who thrive and flourish demonstrate stronger academic performance" (Norrish, Williams, O'Connor, & Robinson, 2013). Students with high wellbeing gain higher grades and lower rates of absence (Suldo, Thalji, & Ferron, 2011), as well as higher self-control and lower procrastination (Howell, 2009) and more creative, open-minded thinking (Fredrickson & Branigan, 2005). Indeed, positive education is a complementary goal, rather than a competing goal with academic performance. More and more schools seem to be prepared to embrace positive education. This research seems to support what many of the best educators have experienced anecdotally- with more than 90% of teachers agreeing that social-emotional learning is helpful for students (Civic Enterprises, 2013).

For many schools, positive education is the missing piece of the puzzle for developing their staff and students, so they can take more productive and deliberate steps on their journey of thriving.

Martin Seligman has created an acronym for the elements of positive psychology: PERMA. It is outlined in his book, Flourish (Seligman, 2011). The elements are: positive emotion (the pleasant life – happiness and life satisfaction); engagement (flow); relationships (other people); meaning (belonging to, or serving, something bigger than ourselves); and accomplishment (success, achievement and mastery). Each of these contributes to our wellbeing, or what Seligman refers to as our level of "flourishing". Each of these can be developed.

It is easy to pass the blame for the rising rates of depression, anxiety and stress: we can blame the government, unions, our employer or our boss. However, playing the victim won't help. And it won't help the students in our classrooms to thrive, flourish and enhance their wellbeing either. Instead, we need to step up and take charge of our wellbeing. We can make it a priority in our lives and our students' lives. We can cultivate our own wellbeing, or experience a decline based on the demands the world makes of us.

Wellbeing training for families and schools

Wellbeing can be cultivated through some very practical training methods. Schools are uniquely placed to promote the wellbeing of young people at a critical stage in their development. In this section I will outline some of the most useful methods I have found so far in my work with school staff and students. The list is not exhaustive, or detailed in full. However, it is intended to give educators and parents a framework and a few ideas. Each of these sections is just as relevant to the parent as it is to the child, and just as relevant to the teacher as it is to the student. Most of these activities can be revisited very regularly, require little or very few resources and only take a short time. They are all based on evidence that links them to increased wellbeing, or directly to improved academic or other life outcomes. We need these aspects in our own lives for our own sakes, but through modelling and teaching them, we pass them on and help kids thrive. For students, the methods will enhance academic outcomes and lead to greater success in other areas of life. The useful and evidence-based areas of wellbeing training covered here are: meditation, character strengths, gratitude and interpersonal skills including active-constructive responding and generosity.

MEDITATION

There are significant physical and psychological benefits of meditation. There is a wealth of evidence that demonstrates the effects meditation has on managing stress, combatting heart disease, lowering blood pressure, boosting our immune systems, building our defence against cancer, slowing the rate at which we age, improving our mood, raising our awareness, and increasing attention and clarity (Michie, 2008; Davidson, et al., 2003). Other benefits include reducing fear, anxiety, depression and anger. These benefits come about as a result of the adaptation of the brain over time, due to the brain activity associated with meditation. These benefits have been found to last much longer than the meditation session itself, because it changes some of the default settings in our brain (Brewer, et al., 2011). Most of these benefits are related to the increased activity in the prefrontal cortex as a direct result of meditation. It has been noted that both the thickness of the pre-frontal cortex and the density of grey matter increases as a result of meditation (Lazar, et al., 2005; Davidson & Lutz, 2008). All of these very well documented changes are collectively termed "the relaxation response" (Benson, 1997).

Meditation takes our thinking out of the past or the future and aims to bring us into the present moment. If it was a drug that we could purchase over the counter it would be a best seller – with so many benefits and no side-effects. When I explain meditation to students, I ask them to imagine that they have a Ferrari of a mind. If they are driving around constantly in a Ferrari, they will sometimes need to refuel. They would need to park the car, put the handbrake on and add fuel, oil and fluid from time to time. Our mind is rushing around constantly, thinking about the past or anticipating the future. We have so many intellectual demands and so many stimuli each day that the mind doesn't naturally get much respite. I tell students to put the hand brake on and refuel. Park the Ferrari that is their mind. It doesn't take long, it doesn't cost them anything, and the benefits are supported by a huge body of evidence. For educators and parents, we should do this for our own sake. Once we do, we will want to share it with the children in our care.

While the thought of teaching meditation to a roomful of students might be off-putting for many educators, I have found that kids are usually very receptive. However, it must be framed well. I have had success leading a "breathing meditation" for almost 200 students at one time in school halls. A note of caution however: I never tell them that we are doing "meditation". That will be sure to disengage those students who think it is a weird thing that only yogis and monks do. There is a process to follow. I have found that by giving the kids instructions without naming it as "mindfulness" or "meditation" they are responsive. Once they have completed the practice, I then explain the benefits of meditation and reveal that they have just done their first meditation. At that point, after the room has been in complete silence and stillness for a few minutes, they seem to believe about the relaxation response and each of the benefits of the practice. After the first attempt, the students are no longer put off by the term meditation, and other techniques can be introduced. At this point, we can look to four of the more common meditation techniques.

Breathing meditation

This meditation involves counting the breath going in and out. For example, breathing in for four counts, pause and breathing out for four counts. Many variations of counts can be used here. For example, breathe in for three, hold for one then breathe out for five. Personally, I think you should find a pattern that works for you and that draws your attention to your breathing without making you uncomfortable. With students, I gently guide them to be able to extend this to six seconds for the in-breath and 6 seconds for the out-breath – roughly five breaths per minute. The suggested time frame for this would depend on the age of the students, however, I usually start with two minutes. I also usually ask students to put one hand, or both hands, on their stomachs, so that they can feel it rising and falling as they inhale and exhale. While I personally do this sort of meditation lying in bed, I like to teach this to students when they are seated with their eyes closed, rather than lying down. The reason for this preference is that it makes it easier to facilitate large groups. It would probably not be necessary in a normal classroom setting.

Body-scan meditation

This meditation is about being aware of different parts of the body in a related sequence. It is not about trying to fix pain or tension, but rather being aware of it and accepting it. It is best taught to students lying down on their back, with their eyes closed. A body-scan meditation usually follows a process of drawing awareness to different parts of the body, in a related sequence. Participants draw their attention and focus to a part of the body and notice the sensations in that area, before moving on to the next area. It is a useful way of drawing the focus away from the past and future happenings in our mind, and drawing ourselves into our body at the present time. Teachers and parents can adequately guide students through this with minimal training.

Mindfulness meditation

This meditation is centred on the idea of being mindful. Rather than following any thoughts that come into our Ferrari of a mind, we simply let them go and keep coming back to the breath. We are mindful of the air coming in through our nostrils. As we inhale, we notice that our stomach rises (much like a balloon that inflates as the air goes into it). As we exhale, the stomach falls. Students can do this meditation sitting or lying down, but they should place one or both hands on their stomach, to assist them in being present to the rise and fall of each breath.

Other examples of mindfulness include mindful walking, eating or breathing. We can simply go about our daily activities mindfully, which allows us to welcome and accept our current state, rather than focus on past disappointments or future worries (Kabat-Zinn, 2003).

Loving kindness meditation (LKM)

Of all the types of meditation, loving kindness has been found to have the greatest impact on increasing our positive emotions. Through loving and kind concern for the wellbeing of all other people, it has been found to broaden attention, enhance positive emotions and reduce negative emotional states while increasing empathy and compassion. LKM is considered particularly helpful for people who have a tendency toward hostility or anger (Analayo, 2003). LKM consists of directing love and kindness "towards oneself, toward specific others or in all directions to all beings" (Hofmann, Grossman, & Hinton, 2011).

While this may be difficult to facilitate with large groups of students, it is quite simple to lead a class group in this meditation. In addition, it is very worthwhile on a personal level. The method requires us to simply bring the body into stillness and focus attention on the breath. Then attention is turned towards oneself. We simply offer love and kindness to ourselves (We might offer a statement to ourselves, such as "May I be happy, may I be at peace, and may I be held in deep compassion"). Then we offer the same to someone we hold close to our hearts. Then we offer love and kindness to someone we find difficult. The final part of the process is offering love and kindness to all human beings, including those we do not know.

While each of these meditations will take an investment of time to establish expectations with groups of students, the time required lessens over time. It should also be noted that each of the descriptions above are brief and simple, just to give you an idea of the process for each. Smiling Mind has a great app and some wonderful YouTube clips with age appropriate meditation techniques that teachers and parents can access for free.

The benefits of meditation are significant and well-researched. It is as useful for adults, as it is to children and can be taught with little time. In fact, I would suggest that two minutes of meditation at the start, or at the half way point, of a 90 minute (double) lesson, would actually increase time on task. In addition, it will increase the quality of work, the attention and focus of the students and lead to greater wellbeing.

CHARACTER STRENGTHS

Strengths are ways of thinking, feeling and behaving that come naturally and easily to a person and which enable high functioning and performance (Linley & Harrington, 2004). While talents are valued for their tangible outcomes, character strengths are valued for moral or intrinsic reasons (Peterson & Seligman, 2004). Character strengths can be used to enhance wellbeing, overcome challenges and nurture relationships (Park, Peterson, & Seligman, 2004). In addition, by developing character strengths in our students, they become better equipped to make valuable contributions to society (Park & Peterson, 2006). Seligman and Peterson devised and validated the values in action (VIA) signature strengths survey, which measures 24 character strengths. This allows people to identify some of their key character strengths and use them accordingly. As with the growth mindset, we must avoid rigid conceptions of ourselves and instead consider our strengths as capable of being improved (Dweck, 2006).

Research has shown that using our top five strengths on a regular basis increases our wellbeing. These are referred to by Seligman and Peterson as our signature strengths. In particular, individuals who were able to use their signature strengths in new ways during a one week trial were found to be happier and less depressed at one month and six month follow-ups (Seligman, Steen, & Peterson, 2005). Furthermore, individuals who use their strengths tend to report greater vitality and psychological wellbeing, and they make more progress towards their goals (Linley, Nielsen, Wood,

& Biswas-Diener, 2010) and experience enhanced resilience after stressful events (Peterson & Seligman, 2003).

One reason that character strengths are so powerful for wellbeing is that humans experience a negativity bias. We have a tendency to focus on negative stimuli more strongly than positive stimuli, thereby making us more aware of our weaknesses and flaws, than our strengths (Baumeister, Bratslavsky, Finkenauer, & Vohs, 2001). Furthermore, because we so consistently act with our strengths, we are often not consciously aware of them and this creates a blind spot (Biswas-Diener, Kashdan, & Minhas, 2010). So it is not surprising that identifying, articulating and intentionally developing our strengths contributes positively to our wellbeing.

The 24 character strengths are characterised under six broad areas, known as virtues. These are: wisdom and knowledge (creativity, curiosity, open-mindedness, love of learning and perspective); courage (honesty, bravery, persistence and zest); humanity (kindness, love and social intelligence); justice (fairness, leadership and teamwork); temperance (forgiveness, modesty, prudence and self-regulation); and transcendence (appreciation of beauty and excellence, gratitude, hope, humour and religiousness/spirituality) (Peterson & Seligman, 2004). You can take the online survey and find out more about these specific character strengths at http://www.viacharacter.org/www/#nav. A youth survey, as well as an adult survey, has been developed in order to help people aged 13 and over engage in a process of self-examination of their own strengths. Once the survey has been completed, respondents are provided with a summary of their top five (signature) strengths, and this represents a suitable starting point for applying and evolving these strengths further.

A character strengths approach can be implemented with staff and students; it will lead to increased self-awareness and awareness of others. Teachers should first identify their own strengths and how they could utilise them more on a daily basis. Teachers can then implement a similar process with students.

The process is as follows: complete the relevant VIA Signature Strengths survey online and access the personalised report; reflect on the use of strengths through writing briefly about a time when we engaged these strengths; share personal signature strengths with others; brainstorm, discover, explore and finally practise ways to continue to utilise and develop these strengths. Useful suggestions for how each strength could be applied, is available on the VIA Strengths website (Rashid, 2015). For staff, this process could be launched in only two short staff meetings on the topic. For students, the launch takes two sequential pastoral care/wellbeing lessons. Not only does this process help the individual and their social connections to other people in the community, it also contributes to the wellbeing, success and thriving of the whole community.

It is clear from the research that identifying and applying our character strengths every day contributes to our wellbeing. In practice, schools are already equipped to lead a focused process of learning about character strengths in order to help the whole community on its journey of thriving.

GRATITUDE

Few things in life are as integral to our wellbeing as gratitude (Emmons, 2007). Gratitude trains our brain to scan our environment and focus on the positive. When we are looking for things to be grateful for, we tend to find them. I referred to this in the earlier section on goal setting and the reticular activation system. Psychologists call this process of priming your brain to remain on the lookout for opportunities as "predictive encoding". They have found that priming your brain to expect a favourable outcome, actually encodes your brain to recognise the outcome when it arises (Siefert & Patalano, 2001). In the words of Henry David Thoreau, "It's not what you look at that matters – it's what you see". People who choose to be grateful wire themselves for more joy, opportunity and positivity. So it is worthwhile to be a "glass-half-full" sort of person.

While religions and philosophies have long embraced gratitude as an essential ingredient to wellbeing and thriving, scientists have been late to recognise this concept. However, there is a growing body of evidence revealing the many benefits of gratitude. Daily gratitude practice resulted in higher reported levels of positive states such as alertness, enthusiasm, determination, attentiveness and energy (Emmons, n.d.). In addition, gratitude correlates with goal attainment, high energy, positive moods, quality of sleep and more positive attitudes towards school and family (Emmons & McCullough, 2003). However, Brene Brown at the University of Houston says that having an "attitude of gratitude" or simply "feeling grateful" isn't enough. Instead we require tangible gratitude practices such as gratitude journals, gratitude jars, gratitude letters and family gratitude rituals (Brown, 2012). There are some simple practices that parents, educators and students can do to cultivate gratitude in our lives. I will share two examples I regularly use with students.

Writing a gratitude letter

Research conducted in 2005 reported that participants who participated in a "gratitude visit" condition were happier and less depressed than a placebo control group. In fact, out of five different conditions offered in the study, the gratitude visit resulted in the largest immediate positive changes (Seligman, Steen, & Peterson, 2005). I have adapted this exercise so that students write a gratitude letter to someone who has been influential and important in their lives. With the right framing, it is wonderful to see kids of all shapes and sizes taking time to be grateful to someone else. I must stress the need for the environment, conditions and expectations to be set up properly, in order to ensure the students are "framed" to participate successfully in this activity. When the session is over, the students are asked to deliver and read the letter to the person for whom it was intended. I have found this a useful way to encourage kids to increase their personal wellbeing through gratitude, and also to express their appreciation for someone else in their lives. Research shows that "gratitude is important for forming and maintaining the most important relationships of our lives – those with the people we interact with every day" (Algoe, 2012) Shawn Achor offers a variation on this where he invites executives and office workers to write a short email each morning to someone in order to express their appreciation – it could be a friend, family member or colleague (Achor, 2010).

"Three good things" or "What went well" activity

This activity involves journaling three things that we are grateful for. Personally, I have found this to be the simplest, most practical way to practise gratitude each day. Each night before bed, I simply recall three things from the day that I am grateful for – it might be a hug from my son when I arrived back from work, an exciting new partnership with a school, the meal that we enjoyed at dinner time or an activity we enjoyed as a family. Regardless of the research, it is an experience that I value and look forward to every day. Maybe that is because I know that there is a huge body of research behind gratitude, and also that this particular practice has been proven to make us happier and less depressed. In a study where participants were explicitly told to continue the practice for one week, the benefits were still noticeable six months afterwards. The researchers suggest the reason for this is because the activity is simple and easy to adhere to (Seligman, Steen, & Peterson, 2005). This meant that participants in the study were likely to continue this practice after they noticed the benefits. So find a time to do this and try it for yourself – starting today. You can do it any time of day. You may like to use what you know about habit formation. You can attach the routine of gratitude to an existing trigger (such as going to bed, eating dinner, brushing your teeth or getting out of bed in the morning). A variation on this activity is to write a short journal entry about a positive experience you have had. One study compared the journaling group to a control group and found that the journaling group were happier and showed less symptoms of illness three months later.

INTERPERSONAL SKILLS

Employers are looking for more than just a cubicle worker these days. After analysing many studies on happiness over the last few decades, researches have concluded that "like food and air, we seem to need social relationships to thrive" (Diener & Biswas-Diener, 2008). Our relationships with other people matter. Researchers have found the factor that distinguished the happiest 10 percent of people from everyone else was the strength of their social relationships (Diener & Seligman, 2002). When we make positive social connections, our body releases oxytocin – a pleasure inducing chemical – into our bloodstream. Oxytocin is sometimes referred to as "the love drug", as it plays a role in bonding, friendships and orgasms. This is why we can seem to be "in sync" or connected to certain people. Furthermore, oxytocin also reduces our anxiety, improves our concentration and focus and helps some of our bodies' systems to function more effectively. Limited social connectedness is linked to higher rates of depression and more work related stress (Achor, 2010). It seems that investing into a healthy social support network is one of the best things we can do to enhance our own thriving. One useful tool we can use to invest in our relationships is active-constructive responding.

ACTIVE-CONSTRUCTIVE RESPONDING (ACR)

As we know, some young (and not so young) people lack critical social skills that enable them to build healthy relationships. Active constructive responding refers to the way that we respond when someone is sharing something positive with us. How we respond to the good news of others can either build a relationship or undermine it (Seligman, 2011). It can be a useful model for sharing with young people, and provides them with a useful tool for enhancing their relationships. ACR involves responding by offering interest, enthusiasm, support, encouragement and sometimes follow-up questions when someone shares good news. I have also found it to be a useful tool for my own relationships, and one that I need to keep working on in order to get better at ACR.

Below is a hypothetical scenario that demonstrates four different ways of responding to someone who is sharing good news. ACR benefits the individual we are relating to as well as the relationship itself. Conversely, each of the other three types has been shown to have a negative impact on the wellbeing of those sharing the good news and also on the relationship (Gable, Gonzaga, & Strachman, 2006).

Situation: A husband responds to his wife's good news that she is being considered for a promotion.

Active constructive responding	"That is wonderful! I am so happy for you. You would be excellent in that new position." (responding enthusiastically; maintaining eye contact, smiling, displaying positive emotions)
Active destructive responding	"If you get the promotion, you are going to have to be at work all week and on Saturday mornings too." (pointing out the downside; displaying negative nonverbal cues)
Passive constructive responding	"That's nice that you are being considered for the promotion." (happy, but lacking enthusiasm/downplaying; little to no active emotional expression)
Passive destructive Responding	"A promotion, huh? Well, hurry up and get changed so we can get some dinner. I'm starving." (lacking interest, displaying little to no eye contact, turning away, leaving the room)

(Source: http://booksite.elsevier.com/9780123745170/Chapter%204/Chapter_4_Worksheet_4.14.pdf)

ACR is a skill, and just like any other it can be developed with practice. Students can be guided through a process that builds their understanding of ACR, and which gives them time to reflect and record their own responses and then to make adjustments over a period of time. It will enhance their relationships and wellbeing, and ultimately will help them thrive.

GENEROSITY

Generosity is good for us! Generosity can come in many forms. One research study focused on generosity of time (volunteering), money (charity) and in relationships (emotional availability and hospitality). The study surveyed 2,000 people over five years. It found that those people who were more generous were happier, less depressed and healthier. In particular, those who described themselves as "very happy" volunteer an average of almost six hours per month, while those who are "unhappy" volunteered an average of less than 40 mins per month. In addition, depression rates were lower for those participants who donated more than 10 percent of their incomes to charity. And finally, those who were more generous in their relationships (emotionally available and hospitable to others) were much more likely to be in excellent health (48 percent) than those who were not (31 percent) (Smith & Davidson, 2014).

In addition to increasing happiness, health and reducing depression, generosity has been found to be contagious. Receiving help reliably increased the likelihood of being generous towards a stranger. Researchers have found that when we receive an act of kindness, we are quite likely to "pay it forward" (Tsvetkova & Macy, 2014; Jordan, Rand, Arbesman, Fowler, & Christakis, 2013). In essence, when we can demonstrate kindness towards someone it is quite possible that the flow-on effect of our generosity will be much larger than the small generous act we offer. It may, in fact, be passed on. One such report occurred in December 2012, when someone bought a coffee at a drive-thru window (Tim Horton's Coffee

Shop), and paid for their own coffee as well as for the person in the car behind them. The next customer paid for the car behind them, and so on, and for the next 3 hours a total of 228 customers did this (Mallough, 2013). Other such instances of between four and 24 cars paying it forward have been reported by Wendy's, McDonald's, Starbucks, Del Taco, Taco Bell, KFC and Dunkin' Donuts restaurants across the USA (Tsvetkova & Macy, 2014). If it's possible in the USA, it's probable in our lucky country! Generosity has been called contagious, probably as a result of situations like this. When we experience generosity, there seems to be a willingness to pass it on.

Interestingly, while *experiencing* generosity increases our likelihood of being generous, *observing* generous acts directed towards others can lead us to believe that our generosity is no longer needed. As a result, we can be less generous because of what researchers call "the bystander effect" – the typical "someone else will do it" syndrome (Tsvetkova & Macy, 2014). Therefore, if we are to spread our generosity, it may be worth investigating ways of being generous in private, rather than in public and avoiding "the bystander effect".

In schools, this can be created into a small project for students – they might be invited to find one totally unselfish thing to do for someone else who needs a hand. Not only does this benefit the receiver and the giver of generosity – it can spark a generosity cycle within a school (or within a small pocket of the school). Random acts of kindness are often given, however, I am of the opinion that it need not be "random" to have the desired impact. For me, random acts of kindness seem a little superficial and are often more about the person doing the giving. Instead, I believe that "targeted" acts of kindness move us from a focus on ourselves to meeting a genuine need for someone who may require it. These acts are much more personal and meaningful. Targeted acts of kindness can still be done in private. However, they require us to be more intentional about choosing a person and tailoring our generosity towards something that is of value to them. In any case (random or targeted), generosity has benefits for our school community and can contribute to the wellbeing of both staff and students. As parents and educators, it is also helpful on a personal level. Not only should we teach this to kids, we should live it ourselves.

Summary

The journey of my work building wellbeing in schools has been focused on doing so through meditation, gratitude, character strengths and interpersonal skills (particularly active-constructive responding and generosity). There are other elements that contribute to our wellbeing such as optimism and hope, savouring, diet and exercise. However, these are outside the bounds of my work with schools. Instead, I focus on high impact, evidence-based areas that can be broken down and taught through large group (whole cohort or whole staff) training or by classroom teachers. Therefore, I will not attempt to outline the benefits of these additional elements or how they can be best utilised. There are others who are far better equipped in these important areas that also make a significant contribution to wellbeing.

If building wellbeing in a school setting is of interest to you, resources and lesson plans are available at: http://www.unleashingpersonalpotential.com.au/

PART FIVE: EFFECTIVE SCHOOL IMPLEMENTATION

- Live it
- Teach it
- Embed it
- Unleashing personal potential and effective school implementation

The focus of this book has been to raise awareness of educators and parents about the three components of thriving. If building growth mindsets, grit and wellbeing in a school setting is of interest to you, some practical and engaging strategies and support material are available at: http://www.unleashingpersonalpotential.com.au/

"It is generally agreed that for reform to be effective requires the articulation of all key aspects, rather than isolated change" (Pendergast, 2009). An example of this is a recipe for a cake that has 10 ingredients. The chef chooses to use only five of them. No one should be surprised if the cake collapses into a pile of crumbs once it is cooked (De Jong & Chadbourne, 2007). From this perspective, implementing any strategy for school change should be done properly, or not at all.

There are only so many hours in the day, and not everything that is good can be done. Every school must have priorities. "The problem is that our schools are inundated with initiatives, and too many schools try to embrace them all. When everything is a priority, nothing is. Schools have to be selective about where they invest their efforts... [this] requires preventing people from doing good things to give them time to do even better things" (William, 2010). William talks about the bower bird mentality whereby we fill our nests with baubles, so there is no room for any more. Therefore, before we add the three ingredients to thriving, we must remember that our staff do not want something extra to distract them. If it is to have the desired impact, we must work smarter by throwing some things out of the nest and replacing them with more useful things. If thriving is great for kids, schools will make it a priority and they will make room for it in the nest. If it is not, they will continue with the other good things they are already doing and not much will change.

In order for thriving to take hold in a school, all key stakeholders should become engaged: teaching and non-teaching staff, parents and students. Building the capacity of the parents and educators that support thriving school communities is an essential step towards successful implementation. Adults need to live it, teach it, and embed it (Norrish, Williams, O'Connor, & Robinson, 2013). This is the model used at Geelong Grammar. While most schools do not have the financial resources this school has, they are not necessary. As schools cannot do everything, those that prioritise thriving will be able to redirect funds from other areas. I wouldn't imagine that Geelong Grammar had half a million dollars waiting to be spent on something – instead they re-prioritised. A thriving school attracts higher enrolments, thereby attracting further government funding, and in the case of Independent and Catholic schools, additional school fees will be collected. In some cases, a single extra enrolment will be enough to enable the full implementation of thriving at a school. It is not a matter of funding; it is a matter of priority. Principals in schools who are committed to thriving will make it happen for their school community.

There are some difficulties when it comes to SEL implementation. Eighty-one percent of teachers trying to implement SEL state that "lack of reinforcement at home" is a major obstacle. Four out of five (82 percent) of teachers report interest in receiving further training in SEL. While nearly all teachers (88 percent) say that SEL occurs in their school on some level although less than half (44 percent) say that SEL is being taught on a school-wide programmatic basis (Civic Enterprises, 2013). My recommendations would include:

- involving parents in the journey of thriving through school newsletters, emails, relevant training and workshops and social media.
- continuing to develop the capacity of our educators in SEL learning. Teachers must know, understand and implement what they have learned in their own lives if they are to be the best models of SEL for our children.
- a whole-school, systematic approach when it comes to implementing any programs or practices.
- seeking to live it, teach it and embed it

I will now focus on each part of the "live it, teach it, embed it" model.

LIVE IT

If we are serious about helping young people thrive, then as adults, we must first live it.

Recently, I was watching some footage of a skateboarder with the year 10s at a school just outside Brisbane. The footage included some skateboard "wipe outs". In particular, a male skateboarder had experienced a particularly hurtful blow when he misjudged the position of a post – it ended up between his legs! It was intended to be a lesson about getting back up and the resilience required to proceed when every fibre of your being is telling you to stop. However, one fascinating thing emerged as the students laughed at the clip. Many of the boys were laughing and sort of screwing up their faces at the same time. It was as though they could feel the unfortunate skateboarder's pain. I realised I had a very similar response the first time I saw the clip too. Then I remembered watching Australia's funniest home videos when I was growing up. I'm almost ashamed to admit it, but of all of the categories of videos submitted, I used to think the unfortunate injuries were the most hilarious. I also recall grabbing my head, groin, knee, chest or whatever part of me that had been injured in the home video. This is experienced as a result of mirror neurons, which are specialised brain cells that actually sense and then mimic (or mirror) the actions, feelings and sensations of another person (Iacoboni, 2008).

As social creatures, we are actually wired for empathy. If we see something unfortunate happen to someone else, the same set of neurons light up in our brains (Achor, 2010). Studies have shown that when three strangers meet in a room, the most overtly expressive person transmits their mood to the other two people within two minutes (Friedman & Riggio, 1981). Mirror neurons also explain why yawning is contagious.

If we want our students to thrive, our staff must be thriving. The students will mimic what they see. As the teacher has centre stage in the classroom, they are most likely to be mirrored by the students. We know that teachers really do create the classroom culture, and mirror neurons are part of the explanation for this. Staff must live the reality of thriving. They must practise what they preach. The same must be said for parents at home. Kids emulate or mirror the behaviour that they see. As adults, it's probably fair to say that, on average, our lives are a little more complicated and at times more stressful than student's. However, we must set the best possible example for the young people who will mimic us. This is a huge challenge for all educators and parents in the reality of our daily lives.

In order to live the reality of thriving, adults must be equipped with the tools. We must possess a growth mindset, grit and wellbeing. School administrators must educate, train, support and mentor staff in ways that contribute to their thriving. We can make thriving part of the culture.

TEACH IT

Thriving through growth mindsets, grit and wellbeing needs to be explicitly taught. The research regarding the benefits of social emotional learning, combined with the links between the growth mindset, grit and wellbeing in terms of achievement is too strong to ignore. Schools should invest time into social-emotional learning, even though this means taking time out of other classes. Employers, parents and teachers also support the research that these skills are necessary for young people and should be taught.

This can be done either by utilising the expertise of outsiders or by upskilling teachers so they can deliver these lessons themselves. While the second model requires greater time and financial investment initially, it is also a more sustainable model that leads to enhanced teacher capacity. It also enhances the "live it" and "embed it" components of the model. This book has endeavoured to break up each component into smaller, more manageable, pieces that are taught in an explicit way. For example, teachers will have more success creating a couple of lessons about delayed gratification or goal setting than they will focusing on the overarching principle of grit. Rather than teaching wellbeing, a series of lessons may focus on character strengths or gratitude. While grit or wellbeing may be too broad to teach, if they are broken into smaller component parts, it can be achieved. Modules on each or the big three areas that may be helpful for schools can be found at our website. It is also then possible to "map" an appropriate sequence over the course of a few years at school. Many schools are looking at a spiral approach, by targeting areas such as growth mindset early on, and then building grit and wellbeing in a structured sequence.

It should be noted that this process of teaching thriving is proactive, not reactive. While some schools prefer to "put out fires" by delivering what the cohort needs after a problem has been identified, this model rather seeks to focus on working towards thriving. Rather than avoiding what we don't want for kids, thriving is about moving towards what we do want. Proactive steps are required to make this happen and a suitable "spiral", or "thriving" curriculum should be developed with a school's particular identity and nuances taken into account. While it is appropriate to respond to the problems that erupt with particular cohorts, doing so resides outside the "thriving" curriculum.

Since beginning my work in schools through Unleashing Personal Potential, I have at times been asked to target particular behaviours with certain groups of students. While there is merit in this approach, it must take place within a larger, proactive framework of a culture of thriving. It may in fact tell us what strategies students should have been equipped with in the year previously. This is a useful starting point for planning a proactive, spiralling curriculum for thriving. It is worth noting that I am not saying that a targeted approach at single or multiple year levels would not be effective. It will have the desired effect if it involves training of staff and students (and possibly parents), follow-up support and data gathering (to ensure progress is captured and future implementation is informed by the data). However, the targeted approach may be more effective in primary schools or in junior secondary where a small group of teachers can be trained and take ownership for supporting thriving amongst students.

EMBED IT

Embedding the language and messages of thriving into a school culture is non-negotiable if we want to create lasting, meaningful improvement. One of the characteristics required for each of the ingredients to thriving is that they must be able to be applied in our daily interactions with the young people we care about. This makes embedding thriving somewhat easier than the other two components of implementation. If school staff are living and teaching thriving, it will be natural for them to embed it in their daily conversations, interactions and activities. It will become part of them and inseparable from their role. If we want our school community and all of its members to thrive, we must embed thriving into the culture. Our assemblies, conversations, feedback, morning notices, newsletter articles, noticeboards could all be used as tools to embed growth mindsets, grit and wellbeing even more.

The challenge for school leadership is to embed thriving in a way that is flexible enough to allow members to contribute as a result of their personal interest and passion for thriving, while ensuring that efforts are not constructed in ad hoc or silo pieces. While all stakeholders are invited (and encouraged) to join in the journey, support the journey and nurture the journey of the school, the direction of the journey should be set and clearly articulated by leadership. The journey of thriving can be made very visible to the wider community (in terms of marketing and promoting the school), but not before it is visible to all community members and firmly embedded in the culture. Additionally, while the day to day responsibility for the implementation of thriving is likely to be delegated to another staff member on the leadership team, the Principal of the school must support, promote and be an ambassador for this work.

UNLEASHING PERSONAL POTENTIAL (UPP) AND EFFECTIVE SCHOOL IMPLEMENTATION

In my work with schools, I have learned that schools are somewhat similar to each other and yet all are unique. I don't just mean in terms of gender, staff, timetables, uniforms, size, buildings and so on. There are far finer nuances which many educators and parents will be well aware of. As a result, there is no one size fits all for thriving when it comes to living, teaching and embedding it. However, there seem to be a number of useful tools that most schools have found helpful on their journey.

I will clarify a few of the tools that I have developed in response to the schools that are already partners with UPP and which are on their journey to thriving. I have worked alongside schools for a fraction of the time that I have worked in them as a teacher and administrator. However, working alongside schools for a short amount of time has been an enlightening experience and I have learned a great deal. It has been as a result of hearing stories from experienced educators and reflecting on my own journey in, and alongside schools that has led me to develop these tools. As I continue to listen and learn from school leaders and reflect upon, and evaluate, my own practice, it would be reasonable to expect that there will be many more developments that will enhance school implementation in the coming years. However, for now I can only share what has been done to this point and the possible future direction for my work and research.

Staff training

This can be delivered in the form of short (60-90 minute) inputs over a number of staff meetings, when one of the aspects of thriving is tackled at a time. Alternatively, schools may prefer half day and full day workshops for staff to launch into thriving. The purpose is to share some of the research and practice with staff in order to help them understand "why" this is such a vital area for the school. The sessions then focus on building the capacity of staff in particular areas, so they can live it for themselves, teach it and embed it in their daily interactions and activities with students.

Student incursions

These sessions are tailored to meet the needs of each school. The two most effective incursion modes are multiple 45-90 minute workshops or whole-day incursions. The purpose of this incursion is to launch students into thriving by building understanding, skills and application. Any student incursion should be followed up with targeted lessons that continue to build on, and apply the concepts learned.

Information about UPP incursions, including testimonials from many of our school partners can be found here: http://www.unleashingpersonalpotential.com.au/student-training/

THRIVE Online Modules (Lesson Plans for Pastoral Care and Wellbeing)

An UPP incursion (or any other training experience) will be wasted if it stands alone and is never referred to. This happens too often in schools with many initiatives – often as a result of the bower bird mentality and sometimes because there is no further follow-up. If the school is not committed to prioritising the journey of thriving (or any other initiative), the community should not bother investing any time or money into it in the first place. At UPP, we work with schools to help every student become their best (rather than just delivering an engaging, fun training experience).

Therefore, it is necessary for UPP to offer additional support. In order to make this simple for schools, UPP provides evidence-based lessons that are practical, easy to use, engaging and relevant. These lessons are facilitated by classroom teachers, which means they can "stand alone", or be used as a follow-up to an UPP training experience. If the facilitating teachers have received training, the quality of their delivery and the effect it has will be far greater. In addition, posters, checklists and newsletter inserts continue to be developed to help partner schools on their journey of thriving.

Evidence-based, engaging, relevant and easy to use lesson plans are available at: http://www.unleashingpersonalpotential.com.au/online-modules/

Parent education

Parents have a great deal of impact on the development of their kids. Including them in the process adds value to the initiative, builds capacity in them and strengthens the school/home partnership. This allows parents to be active participants in the journey of thriving. Training parents in the components of thriving is a fantastic contributor to positive outcomes for students. The only trouble that some schools face is getting a large number of parents along to parent education sessions. If schools can offer these parent sessions, parents become a catalyst for improvements in thriving. This training is also useful for assisting the school to build its reputation for helping kids to reach their potential.

Survey data

Prior to an UPP incursion or using THRIVE Online Modules, school communities are invited to participate in an online, self-report survey. This survey is based on the work of Carol Dweck, Angela Duckworth and Martin Seligman, and allows UPP and the school to develop some baselines for their work. Further to this, Dr Peggy Kern from University of Melbourne's Centre for Positive Psychology has testified that the UPPMGW survey "is reliable and successfully captures mindset, grit, and wellbeing." In order to ensure that the work leads to thriving and is having the desired impact, it is important to measure and evaluate. A follow-up survey is conducted, which allows schools to understand the impact their initiative has had on levels of growth mindset, grit and wellbeing. There will be many further developments as we seek evidence-based answers to questions such as, "Are some implementation methods more effective than others?" "Does improving results on this particular survey lead to better academic application and performance?" I look forward to the challenges that lie ahead as I work with partner schools on their journey of thriving.

For more information, as well as access to research articles, school testimonials, resources and lesson plans, go to https://www.unleashingpersonalpotential.com.au/

SOME WORDS FOR INSPIRATION

In working with students over the last ten years, there have been a number of pieces of prose that have inspired me. I have included two of my favourite in the hope that these words might impact and encourage others in similar ways.

The first is often erroneously attributed to Nelson Mandela, however it is from Marianne Williamson's book, *A Return to Love* (Williamson, 1992). It strikes a chord with me, both on a personal level and for all of the students who I have taught over the years. If only a few of them hang onto these words, the world will be a better place.

Our deepest fear is not that we are inadequate.

Our deepest fear is that we are powerful beyond measure.

It is our light, not our darkness that most frightens us.

We ask ourselves, Who am I to be brilliant, gorgeous, talented, and fabulous?

Actually, who are you not to be?

You are a child of God. Your playing small does not serve the world.

There is nothing enlightened about shrinking so that other people will not feel insecure around you. We are all meant to shine, as children do.

We were born to make manifest the glory of God that is within us.

It is not just in some of us; it is in everyone and as we let our own light shine, we unconsciously give others permission to do the same.

As we are liberated from our own fear, our presence automatically liberates others.

The second piece is from Oscar Romero. It helps me to understand the small part we can all play as educators and parents in the journey of the young people in our care. We may never see the end results, but we can contribute in part to their thriving.

A Future Not Our Own

It helps now and then to step back and take a long view. The Kingdom is not only beyond our efforts, it is beyond our vision.

We accomplish in our lifetime only a fraction of the magnificent enterprise that is God's work.
Nothing we do is complete, which is another way of saying that the kingdom always lies beyond us.
No statement says all that could be said.
No prayer fully expresses our faith. No confession brings perfection, no pastoral visit brings wholeness.
No program accomplishes the Church's mission.
No set of goals and objectives include everything.

This is what we are about. We plant the seeds that one day will grow. We water the seeds already planted knowing that they hold future promise.
We lay foundations that will need further development.
We provide yeast that produces effects far beyond our capabilities.

We cannot do everything, and there is a sense of liberation in realizing this.
This enables us to do something, and to do it very well.
It may be incomplete, but it is a beginning, a step along the way, an opportunity for the Lord's grace to enter and do the rest.
We may never see the end results, but that is the difference between the master builder and the worker.

We are workers, not master builders, ministers, not messiahs. We are prophets of a future not our own."

Source: (https://educationforjustice.org/pdfs/ej/romero.pdf)

BIBLIOGRAPHY

ACARA. (2013). *General capabilities in the Australian Curriculum-personal and social capability.*

Achor, S. (2010). *The Happiness Advantage.* New York: Random House.

Algoe, S. (2012). Find, Remind, and Bind: The Functions of Gratitude in Everyday Relationships. *Social and Personality Psychology Compass,* 455-469.

American Heritage® Dictionary of the English Language. (2011). Houghton Mifflin Harcourt Company.

Analayo. (2003). *Satipatthana: The direct path to realization.* Birmingham, UK: Windhorse.

Ansel, K. (2009). *Is your diet making you gain?* Retrieved from health.msn: www.health.msn.com.

(2006). *Are they really ready to work? Employers persepectives on the basic knowledge and applied skills of new entrants to the 21st century US workforce.* The Conference Board, Corporate Voices for Working Families, the Partnership for 21st Century Skills and the Society for Human Resource Management.

Aronson, J. (2002). *Improving academic achievement: impact of psychological factors on education.* New York: Academic Press.

Aronson, J., Fried, C., & Good, C. (2002). Reducing the effects of stereotype threat on African American college students by shaping mindsets of intelligence. *Journal of Experimental Social Psychology*, 113-125.

Bancino, R. & Zevalkink, C. (2007). Soft skills: The new curriculum for hard-core technical professionals. *Techniques: Connecting Education and Careers*, 20-22.

Barber, C. (2011, May 18). *Goldilocks communication: Just the right amount of information*. Retrieved from Vivid Method: http://vividmethod.com/goldilocks-communication-just-the-right-amount-of-information/

Battistich, V., Schaps, E., & Wilson, N. (2004). Effects of an Elementary school intervention on students "connectedness" to school and social adjustment during middle school. *The Journal of Primary Prevention*, 15-24.

Baumeister, R., & Tierney, J. (2012). *Willpower: Rediscovering the Greatest Human Strength*. London: Penguin Group.

Baumeister, R., Bratslavsky, E., Finkenauer, C., & Vohs, K. (2001). Bad is stronger than good. *Review of General Psychology*, 323-370.

Benson, H. (1997). The relaxation response: therapeutic effect. *Science*, 1693-1697.

Bernard, M. (2007). *Student social and emotional health report*. Oakleigh, VIC: Australian Scholarships Group.

Binet, A. (1909). *Modern Ideas About Children*. Paris: Flammarion.

Biswas-Diener, R., Kashdan, T., & Minhas, G. (2010). A dynamic approach to psychological strength development and intervention. *Journal of Positive Psychology,* 106-118.

Blackwell, L., Trzesniewski, K., & Dweck, C. (2007). Implicit theories of intelligence predict achievement across an adolescent transition: a longtitudinal study and an intervention. *Child Development,* 246-263.

Bloom, B. (1985). *Developing Talent in young people.* New York: Ballantine Books.

Brewer, J., Worhunsky, P., Gray, J., Tang, Y., Weber, J., & Kober, H. (2011). Meditation experience is associated with differences in default mode network activity and connectivity. *Proceedings of the National Academy of Sciences of the United States of America,* 20254–20259.

Brown, B. (2012). *Daring Greatly: How the Courage to Be Vulnerable Transforms the Way We Live, Love, Parent, and Lead.* New York: Gotham.

Bruel-Jungerman, E., Davis, S., & Laroche, S. (2007). Brain plasticity mechanisms and memory: A part of four. *Neuroscientist,* 492-505.

Byrne, J. (1997). Synaptic Plasticity. *Neuroscience Online.*

Chechik, G., Meilijson I, & Ruppin, E. (1999). Neuronal Regulation: a mechanism for synaptic pruning during brain maturation. *Neural Computation,* 2061-2080.

Civic Enterprises., Bridgeland, J., Bruce, M., & Hariharan, (2013). *The Missing Piece: A National Teacher Survey on How Social and Emotional Learning Can Empower Children and Transform Schools.* Chicago: Collaborative for Academic, Social, and Emotional Learning.

Clear, J. (2014, January). *40 Years of Stanford Research Found That People With This One Quality Are More Likely to Succeed.* Retrieved from Jamesclear.com: http://jamesclear.com/delayed-gratification

Clear, J. (2014). *How to Stick With Good Habits Even When Your Willpower is Gone.* Retrieved from jamesclear.com: http://jamesclear.com/choice-architecture

Clear, J. (2014). *This Coach Improved Every Tiny Thing by 1 Percent and Here's What Happened.* Retrieved from JamesClear.com: http://jamesclear.com/marginal-gains

Cohen, S., Doyle, W., Turner, R., Alper, C., & Skoner, D. (2003). Emotional style and susceptibility to the common cold. *Psychosomatic Medicine,* 652-657.

Csikszentmihayli, M. (1997). *Finding flow: the psychology of engagement in everyday life.* New York: Basic Books.

Daloz, L. (1986). *Effective teaching and mentoring: realizing the transformational power of adult learning experiences.* San Francisco: Jossey-Bass.

Danner, D., Snowdon, D., & Friesen, W. (2001). Positive Emotions in Early Life and Longevity: Findings from the Nun Study. *Journal of Personality and Social Psychology,* 804-813.

Davidson, R., & Lutz, A. (2008). Buddha's Brain: Neuroplasticity and Meditation. *IEEE Signal Processing Magazine.*

Davidson, R., Kabat-Zinn, J., Schumacher, J., Rosenkranz, M., Muller, D., Santorelli, S., Urbanowski F, Harrington A, Bonus K, & Sheridan, J. (2003). Alterations in brain and immune function produced by mindfulness meditation. *Psychosomatic Medicine,* 564-570.

De Jong, T. & Chadbourne, R. (2007). Whole-hog or half-hog: which model for middle schooling? *Australian Journal for MIddle Schooling.*

Diehl, E. (2010, July 2). *Can change happen in a school?* Retrieved from Mindsets in education: http://mindsetsineducation.blogspot.com.au/

Diener, E., & Biswas-Diener, R. (2008). *Happiness: unlocking the mysteries of psychological wealth.* Malden, MA: Wiley-Blackwell.

Diener, E., & Seligman, M. (2002). Very happy people. *Psychological Science,* 81-84.

Diener, E., Nickerson, C., Lucas, R., & Sandvik, E. (2002). Dispositional Affect and Job Outcomes. *Social indicators research,* 229-259.

Doidge, N. (2007). *The Brain That Changes Itself: Stories of personal triumph from the frontiers of brain science.* New York: Penguin Group.

Donahue, J. (n.d.). *The compound effect.* Retrieved from Actionable books: http://www.actionablebooks.com/en-ca/summaries/the-compound-effect/

Duckworth, A. (2013, April). *True Grit.* Retrieved from Association for Psychological Science: http://www.psychologicalscience.org/index.php/publications/observer/2013/april-13/true-grit.html

Duckworth, A. (2007). Grit: perserverance and passion for long-term goals. *Journal of Personality and Social Psychology,* 1087-1101.

Duckworth, A. (2005). Self-discipline outdoes IQ in predicting academic performance of adolescents. *Psychological Science,* 939-944.

Duckworth, A., Grant, H., Loew, B., Oettingen, G., & Gollwitzer, P. (2011). Self-regulation strategies improve self-discipline in adolescents: benefits of mental contrasting and implementation intentions. *Educational Psychology,* 17-26.

Duhigg, C. (2013). *The Power of Habit.* London: Random House Books.

Durlak, J., Weissberg, R., Dymnicki, A., Taylor, R., & Schellinger, K (2011). The impact of enhancing students social and emotional learning: a meta-analyses of school based universal interventions. *Child Development,* 405-432.

Dweck, C. (2006). *Mindset: The new psychology of success.* New York: Ballantine Books.

Dweck, C. (2009). *Theories of Intelligence.* Retrieved from education.com: http://www.education.com/reference/article/theories-of-intelligence/

Eccles, J., Wigfield, A., and Schiefele, U. (2001). Motivation to succeed. In N. Eisenberg, *Handbook of Child Psychology* (pp. 1017-1095). New York: Wiley.

Elias, M., Zins, J., Weissberg, R., Frey, K., Greenberg, M., Haynes, N., Kessler, R., Schwab-Stone, M., and Shriver, T. (1997). *Promoting social and emotional learning: guidelines for educators.* Alexandira, VA: Association for Supervision and Curriculum Development.

Emmons, R. (2007). *Thanks! How the new science of gratitude can make you happier.* New York: Houghton Mifflin.

Emmons, R. (n.d.). *Gratitude and wellbeing.* Retrieved from Emmons Lab: http://emmons.faculty.ucdavis.edu/gratitude-and-well-being/

Emmons, R., & McCullough, M. (2003). Counting blessings versus burdens: An experimental investigation of gratitude and subjective well-being in daily life. *Journal of Personality and Social Psychology,* 377-389.

Ericsson, K., Krampe, R., & Tesch-Romer, C. (1993). The Role of Deliberate Practice in the Acquisition of Expert Performance. *Psychological Reveiw,* 363-406.

Ericsson, K., Prietula, M., & Cokely, E. (2007). The making of an expert. *Harvard Business Review,* 115-121.

Fredrickson, B., & Branigan, C. (2005). Positive emotions broaden the scope of attention and thought- action repertoires. *Cognition and Emotion,* 313-332.

Friedman, H., & Riggio, R. (1981). Effect of individual differences in nonverbal expressiveness on transmission of emotion. *Journal of nonverbal behaviour,* 96-104.

Fullan, M. (2013). *Great to excellent: lanching the next stage of Ontario's educational agenda.* Ontario.

Gable, S., Gonzaga, G., & Strachman, A. (2006). Will you be there when things go right? Supportive responses to positive event disclosures. *Journal of Personality and Social Psychology,* 904-917.

Giedd, J. (2009, February 26). *The Teen Brain- Primed to learn, Primed to take risks.* Retrieved from The Dana Foundation: http://www.dana.org/Cerebrum/2009/The_Teen_Brain__Primed_to_Learn,_Primed_to_Take_Risks/

Gladwell, M. (2008). *Outliers-the story of success*. London: Penguin Books.

Goleman, D. (1998). *Working with emotional intelligence*. New York: Bantam.

Goleman, D. (2006). *Social intellignence: the new science of human relationships*. London: Hutchinson.

Gollwitzer, P. (1999). Implementation intentions: strong effects of simple plans. *American Psychologist*, 493-503.

Good, C., Aronson, J., & Inzlicht, M. (2003). Improving adolescents' standardized test performance: An intervention to reduce the effects of stereotype threat. *Applied Developmental Psychology*, 645 – 662.

Grammar, G. (n.d.). *What is positive education?* Retrieved from Geelong Grammar: https://www.ggs.vic.edu.au/School/Positive-Education/What-is-Positive-Education

Gunderson, E., Gripshover, S., Romero, C., Dweck, C., Goldin-Meadow, S., & Levine, S. (2013). Parent Praise to 1- to 3-Year-Olds Predicts Children's Motivational Frameworks 5 Years Later. *Child Development*, 1-16.

Hattie, J. (2009). *Visible Learning: a synthesis of over 800 meta-analyses related to learning*. Oxon: Routledge.

Hill, N. (1937). *Think and Grow Rich*. Los Angeles, USA: Wilshire Book Company.

Hofmann, S., Grossman, P., & Hinton, D. (2011). Loving-kindness and compassion meditation: Potential for psychological interventions. *Clinical Psychology Review*, 1126-1132.

Hong, Y. Dweck, C., Chiu, C., Lin, D., & Wan, W. (1999). Implicit theories, attributions and coping: a meaning system approach. *Journal of Personaility and Social Psychology,* 588-599.

Howell, A. (2009). Flourishing: achievement-related correlates of students wellbeing. *Journal of Positive Psychology,* 1-13.

Iacoboni, M. (2008). *Mirroring people.* New York: Picador.

Iglesias, J., Eriksson, J., Grize, F., Tomassini, M., & Villa, A. (2005). Dynamics of pruning in simulated large-scale spiking neural networks. *BioSystems,* 11-20.

Index, G.-H. W. (2008). *Poll: Unhappy workers take more sick days.* Associated Press.

J.K. Rowling. (2015, April 18). Retrieved from Wikipedia: http://en.wikipedia.org/wiki/J._K._Rowling#Harry_Potter

James, T. (n.d.). *All about reticular activating system.* Retrieved from NLP Coaching: http://www.nlpcoaching.com/all-about-reticular-activating-system/

James, W. (1984). *Psychology: briefer course.* Harvard University Press.

Jordan, J., Rand, D., Arbesman, S., Fowler, J., & Christakis, N. (2013). Contagion of Cooperation in Static and Fluid Social Networks. *PLoS ONE.*

Kabat-Zinn, J. (2003). Mindfulness based interventions in context: past present and future. *Clinical Psychology: Science and Practice,* 144-156.

Kadison, R. (2005). Getting an edge- use of stimulants and antidepressants in college. *New England Journal of Medicine.*

Kaplan, K. (2004). College faces mental health crisis. *The Harvard Crimson.*

Kemenes, I. Straub, V., Nikitin, E., Staras, K., O'Shea, M., Kemenes, G., Benjamin, P. (2006). Role of delayed nonsynaptic neuronal plasticity in long-term associative memory. *Current Biology,* 1269-1279.

Kidd, C., Palmeri, H., & Aslin, R. (2013). Rational snacking: Young children's decision-making on the marshmallow task is moderated by beliefs about environmental reliability. *Cognition,* 109-114.

Kilgard, M., Pandya, P., Vazquez, J.,Gehi, A., Schreiner, C., & Merzenich, M. (2001). Sensory input directs spatial and temporal plasticity in primary auditory cortex. *Journal of Neurophysiology,* 326-338.

Koch, R. (2011). *Living life the 80/20 way.* Nicholas Brealey Publishing.

Lazar, S., Kerr, C., Wasserman, R., Gray, J., Greve, D., Treadway, M., . . . Quinn, B. e. (2005). "Meditation experience is associated with increased cortical thickness". *Neuroreport,* 1893-1897.

Levitin, D. (2007). *This Is Your Brain on Music: The Science of a Human Obsession.* Plume Books.

Linley, A., & Harrington, S. (2004). Playing to your strengths. *Psychologist,* 86-89.

Linley, A., Nielsen, K., Wood, A. G., & Biswas-Diener, R. (2010). Using signature strengths in pursuit of goals: effects on goal progress, need satisfaction, and wellbeing, and implication for coaching psychologists. *International Coaching Psychology Review,* 8-17.

Lyubomirsky, S., King, L., & Diener, E. (2005). The Benefits of Frequent Positive Affect: Does Happiness Lead to Success? *Psychological Bulletin,* 803-855.

Magan, E., Dweck, C., & Gross, J. (2008). The Hidden-Zero Effect. Representing a Single Choice as an Extended Sequence. Reduces Impulsive Choice. *Psychologoical Science,* 648-649.

Mallough, R. (2013, January 16). *An extra-large sized order of generosity.* Retrieved from Macleans: http://www.macleans.ca/news/canada/an-extra-large-sized-order-of-generosity/

Mark, G., Gudith, D., & Klocke, U. (2008). *The Cost of Interrupted Work: More Speed and Stress.*

Michie, D. (2008). *Hurry up and meditate.* Crows Nest: Alen & Unwin.

Ministerial Council for Education, Employment, Training and Youth Affairs. (2008). *Melbourne Declaration on the Educational Goals for young Australians.*

Mischel, W. (1958). Preference for delayed reinforcement: An experimental study of a cultural observation. *The Journal of Abnormal and Social Psychology,* 57-61.

Mischel, W., & Ebeensen, E. (1970). Attention in delay of gratification. *Jounral of Personality and Social Psychology,* 329-337.

Mischel, W., Ebbensen, E., & Raskoffe, A. (1972). Cognitive and attentional mechanisms in delay of gratification. *Journal of Personality and Social Psychology,* 204-218.

Mischel, W., Shoda, Y., & Rodriguez, M. (1989). Delay of gratification in children. *Science,* 933-938.

Mueller, C., & Dweck, C. (1996). *Implicit theories of intelligence: Relation of parental beliefs to children's expectations.* Poster session presented at Head Start's Third National Research Conference. Washington, DC.

Mueller, C., & Dweck, C. (1998). Intelligence praise can undermine motivation and performance. *Journal of Personality and Social Psychology,* 33-52.

Musch, J., & Grondin, S. (2001). Unequal Competition as an Impediment to Personal Development: A Review of the Relative Age Effect in Sport. *Developmental Review,* 147-167.

Nagel, M. C. (2012). *In the beginning: The brain, early development and learning.* Melbourne: ACER Press.

Neal, D., Wood, W., & Quinn, J. (2006). Habits—A Repeat Performance. *Current Directions in Psychological Science,* 198-202.

Norrish, J., Williams, P., O'Connor, M., & Robinson, J. (2013). An applied framework for positive psychology. *International Journal of Wellbeing,* 147-161.

NRL *Player Birthdays.* (n.d.). Retrieved from Zero Tackle: http://www.zerotackle.com/nrl/rugby-league/players/birthdays/see-all/

Oettingen, G., Mayer, D., Sevincer, A., Stephens, E., Pak, H., & Hagenah, M. (2009). Mental contrasting and goal commitment: the mediating role of energization. *Personality and Psychology Bulletin,* 608-622.

Once upon my time. (2015, April 16). Retrieved from 3 ways to help your kid ace the marshmallow test: http://blog.onceuponmytime. com/3-ways-to-help-your-kid-ace-the-marshmallow-test/#note-174-6

Palmer, P. (1998). *The Courage to Teach.* Boston: Jossey-Bass.

Park, N., & Peterson, C. (2006). Moral competence and character strengths among adolescents: The development and validation of the Values in Action Inventory of Strengths for Youth. *Journal of Adolescence,* 891-909.

Park, N., Peterson, C., & Seligman, M. (2004). Strengths of character and wellbeing. *Journal of Social and Clinical Psychology,* 603-619.

Pascual-Leone, A., Amedi, A., Fregni, F., & Merabet, L. (2005). The plastic human brain cortex. *Annual Review of Neuroscience,* 377-401.

Pascual-Leone, A., Freitas, C., Oberman, L., Horvath, JC., Halko, M., Eldaief, M., Bashir, S., Vernet, M., Shafi, M., Westover, B., Vahabzadeh-Hagh, A., Rotenberg, A. (2011). Characterising brain cortical plasticity and network dynamics across the age-span in health and disease with TMS-EEG and TMS-fMRI. *Brain Topography,* 302-315.

Pendergast, D. (2009). The success of middle years initiatives. *Professional Voice,* 13-17.

Peterson, C., & Seligman, M. (2003). *Character strengths before and after September 11. Psychological Science*, 381-384.

Peterson, C., & Seligman, M. (2004). *Character strengths and virtues: a handbook and classification.* New York: Oxford University Press & Washington DC: American Psychological Association.

Program, U. N. (1992). 1992 *Human Development Report.* New York: Oxford University Press.

Rashid, T. (2015). *340 Ways.* Retrieved from VIA Institute on Character: http://www.viacharacter.org/www/Reports-Courses-Resources/340-Ways?trk_msg=J4TSPMB4TJ4K9AVRBOI9 ULNEFC&trk_contact=KT60CDVCGAO8U477GP0HM NJEQG&utm_source=Listrak&utm_medium=Email&utm_ term=http%3a%2f%2fwww.viacharacter.org%2fwww%2fReports-Courses-Resources%2

reachout.com. (2014). *Embracing the F word.* Retrieved from reachout.com: http://au.professionals.reachout.com/-/media/ pdf/professionals/teachers/embracing%20the%20f%20word%20 classroom%20resource/sp0348embracingthefword_web-3.pdf

Rheault, M., & McGeeney, K. (2011). Emotional health higher among older Americans. *Gallup Wellbeing.*

Rhodewalt, F. (1994). Conceptions of ability, achievement goals, and individual differences in self-handicapping behavior: On the application of implicit theories. *Journal of Personality,* 67-85.

Riggio, R. (2010). Why happiness at work is declining. *Psychology Today.*

Robinson, K., & Aronica, L. (2009). *The Element.* London: Penguin Books.

Rooney, P. (2002, October 3). Microsoft's CEO: 80-20 rule applies to bugs, not just features.

Rotter, J. (1966). Generalized expectancies for internal versus external control of reinforcements. *Psychological Monographs.*

Sala, C., Cambianica, I., & Rossi, F. (2008). Molecular mechanisms of dendritic spine development and maintenance. *Acta Neurobiologiae Experimentalis,* 289-304.

Sawyer, M. A. (2000). *The mental health of young people in Australia.* Commonwealth Department of Health and Aged Care.

Seligman, M. (2002). *Authentic Happiness.* New York: Free Press.

Seligman, M. (2011). *Flourish: a visionary new understanding of happiness and wellbeing.* New York: Simon & Schuster.

Seligman, M., Steen, T., & Peterson, C. (2005). *Positive Psychology Progress: Empirical Validation of Interventions.*

Shoda, Y., Mischel, W., & Peake, P. (1990). "Predicting Adolescent Cognitive and Self-Regulatory Competencies from Preschool Delay of Gratification: Identifying Diagnostic Conditions. *Developmental Psychology,* 978-986.

Siefert, C., & Patalano, A. (2001). Opportunism in memory: preparing for chance encounters. *Current Directions in Psychological Science,* 198-201.

Smith, C., & Davidson, H. (2014). *The Paradox of Generosity: Giving We Receive, Grasping We Lose.* New York: Oxford University Press.

Stafford, K. M. (2007). *Proving and improving*. Newcastle: Hunter Institute of Mental Health.

Staw, B., Sutton, R., & Pelled, L. (1994). Employee positive emotions and favourable outcomes at the workplace. *Organisational Science*, 51-71.

Sternberg, R. (2003). *Wisdom, intelligence and creativity synthesised*. New York: Cambridge University Press.

Suldo, S., Thalji, A., & Ferron, J. (2011). Longtitudinal academic outcomes predicted by ealy adolescents subjective wellbeing, psychopathology and mental health status yielded from a dual factor model. *Journal of Positive Psychology*, 17-30.

Thompson, C. (2005, October 16). *Meet the Life Hackers*. Retrieved from The New York Times: http://www.nytimes.com/2005/10/16/magazine/16guru.html?pagewanted=all

Thorndike, A., Sonnenberg, L., Riis, J., Barraclough, S., & Levy, D. (2012). A 2-phase labeling and choice architecture intervention to improve healthy food and beverage choices. *American Journal of Public Health*, 527-33.

Tsvetkova, M., & Macy, M. (2014). The Social Contagion of Generosity. *PLoS ONE*.

Val, E., & Linley, P. (2006). Posttraumatic Growth, Positive Changes, and Negative Changes in Madrid Residents following the March 11, 2004, Madrid Train Bombings. *Journal of Loss and Trauma: International Perspectives on Stress & Coping*, 409-424.

Vanderhaegen, P. C. (2010). Guidance Molecules in Axon Pruning and Cell Death. *Cold Spring Harbor Perspectives in Biology*, 1-18.

Walsh, F. (2002). Bouncing forward: resilience in the aftermath of September 11. *Family Processes, 34-36.*

Weiss, T. (2002). Posttraumatic Growth in Women with Breast Cancer and Their Husbands: An Intersubjective Validation Study. *Journal of Psychosocial Oncology,* 65-80.

William, D. (2010). Teacher quality: how to get more of it. *Spectator 'Schools Revolution' conference.* London: Institute of Education.

William, D. (2011). *Embedded Formative Assessment - practical strategies and tools for K-12 teachers.* Bloomington: Solution Tree Press.

Williamson, M. (1992). *A return to love.* Harper One.

Willingham, W. (1985). *Success in college: The role of personal qualities and academic ability.* New York: College Entrance Examination Board.

Wilma Rudolph. (2015, April 11). Retrieved from Wikipedia: http://en.wikipedia.org/wiki/Wilma_Rudolph

Wood, W., Quinn, J., & Kashy, D. (2002). Habits in Everyday Life: The Thought and Feel of Action. *Journal of Personality and Social Psychology,* 1281–1297.

Wood, W., Quinn, J., & Kashy, D. (2002). Habits in everyday life: Thought, emotion, and action. *Journal of Personality and Social Psychology,* 1281-1297.

Woodcock, K. (2010). *Safety evaluation techniques.* Toronto: Ryerson University.

Yurgelun-Todd, D., & Killgore, W. (2006). Fear-related activity in the prefrontal cortex increases with age during adolescence: A preliminary fMRI study. *Neuroscience Letters,* 194-199.

Zimbardo, P. (1985). *Psychology and life.* Boston: Ally & Bacon.

Zins, J., Bloodworth, M., Weissberg, R., & Walberg, H. (2007). The scientific base linking emotional learning to school success. *Journal of Educational and Psychological Consultation,* 191-210.

Printed in Australia
AUHW011501021118
304708AU00006B/9